"BEAUTIFUL ILLUSTRATIONS EMPHASIZING THE POWERFUL WORDS THAT HAVE ENTHRALLED FOR MILLENNIA AND WILL CONTINUE TO DO SO FOR MANY MORE."

MIKE PERKINS
AWARD-WINNING ILLUSTRATOR,
MARVEL COMICS

"BRINGS CONTEMPORARY SENSIBILITIES AND A SUPERHERO TONE TO CLASSIC BIBLICAL TALES."

CLIFF BIGGERS
COMIC BOOK NEWS

"BEAUTIFUL AND IMPRESSIVE."

DAVID LLOYD
ACES WEEKLY

THE LION COMIC BOOK HERO BIBLE

SIKU, RICHARD THOMAS & JEFF ANDERSON

LION

CONTENTS

OLD TESTAMENT

NEW TESTAMENT

IN THE BEGINNING
GOD CREATED THE HEAVENS AND THE EARTH.
GOD SAID...
KABOOM!
LET THERE BE...
AND THERE WAS.
LET US MAKE MAN IN OUR IMAGE.
MAN WAS FORMED FROM THE GROUND AND GIVEN THE BREATH OF LIFE. GOD CALLED HIM ADAM...EARTHMAN.
EARTHMAN WAS THE ULTIMATE CREATURE IN GOD'S CREATION.

GOD CREATED A SPECIAL GARDEN, THE GARDEN OF EDEN, WHERE HE AND EARTHMAN COULD MEET.
AND ALL WAS WELL BETWEEN GOD AND HIS CREATION.
EARTHMAN NAMED ALL THE ANIMALS, BUT HE FOUND NO COMPANION FOR HIMSELF.
EARTHMAN WAS ALONE.
IT IS NOT GOOD FOR MAN TO BE ALONE.
WHILE EARTHMAN SLEPT, GOD TOOK ONE OF HIS RIBS AND CREATED EVE, **WOMAN**.

EARTHMAN AWOKE TO SEE THE WOMAN GOD HAD CREATED.
IT WAS LOVE AT FIRST SIGHT.
YOU ARE FLESH OF MY FLESH AND BONE OF MY BONES.
SHE WAS PERFECT.
EARTHMAN NOW HAD HIS COMPANION.

VENOM
IN THE MIDDLE OF THE GARDEN WAS THE TREE OF THE KNOWLEDGE OF GOOD AND EVIL. GOD HAD TOLD EARTHMAN NOT TO EAT FROM IT.
ONE DAY WOMAN GAZED AT THE FRUIT ON THE TREE.
DID GOD REALLY FORBID YOU TO EAT THIS GOOD FRUIT? IT WILL NOT HARM YOU. IT WILL JUST MAKE YOU WISE, LIKE GOD.
TAKE, EAT, AND ENJOY!

BEGUILED BY THE SERPENT, WOMAN ATE THE FRUIT.
EARTHMAN WAS THERE AND SAW WHAT HAPPENED.
WOMAN GAVE THE FRUIT TO HIM TO EAT AS WELL.
THEIR EYES WERE OPENED WIDE.
AND THEY REALIZED THAT THEY WERE NAKED.

IN THE COOL OF THE DAY...
EARTHMAN, WHERE ARE YOU?
UH...I'M OVER HERE.
WHY ARE YOU HIDING?
BECAUSE WE ARE NAKED. WE ATE FROM THE FRUIT OF THE TREE.
YOU HAVE DISOBEYED ME. THE GROUND IS NOW CURSED BECAUSE OF YOU.
GO!
AND GOD DROVE THEM OUT OF EDEN.

PARADISE LOST
BANISHED FROM THE GARDEN, EARTHMAN AND WOMAN LIVED A HARD LIFE, WORKING THE SOIL.
THEY HAD TWO SONS. ABEL BECAME A SHEPHERD, AND HE SACRIFICED TO GOD FROM HIS FLOCK.
HIS OLDER BROTHER, CAIN, WAS A FARMER, AND HE SACRIFICED TO GOD FROM HIS CROP.
GOD WAS PLEASED WITH ABEL AND HIS OFFERING. BUT NOT WITH CAIN.
CAIN WAS FURIOUS.
SO GOD SENT HIM A WARNING.
SIN IS AT YOUR BACK, LURKING. YOU MUST MASTER IT.
JUST DO IT.
CAIN LISTENED TO SIN AND NOT TO GOD. HE MURDERED ABEL.
GOD DROVE CAIN OFF THE SOIL, AWAY FROM HIS PRESENCE. CAIN LIVED OUT HIS LIFE AS A FUGITIVE MAN, EAST OF EDEN.

LAND OF THE GIANTS
AS THE EARTH BECAME MORE POPULATED, THE SONS OF GOD TOOK THE DAUGHTERS OF MEN FOR THEIR BRIDES.
BUT THIS DISPLEASED GOD.
MY SPIRIT SHALL NOT ABIDE WITH MAN FOREVER, FOR HE IS MORTAL. HIS LIFESPAN WILL BE LIMITED.
I WILL DESTROY ALL THE LIVING THINGS I HAVE CREATED. THE WORLD IS FULL OF VIOLENCE BECAUSE OF THEM.
AT THAT TIME, THERE WERE GIANTS ON EARTH. THESE WERE THE GREAT WARRIORS OF OLD, FEARED BY ALL. THE WARRIORS OF RENOWN.
GOD SAW THAT HUMANS WERE WICKED, AND WAS SORRY THAT HE HAD MADE THEM.

RAINMAN
BUT NOAH WAS BLAMELESS, HE FOUND FAVOR IN THE EYES OF GOD.
THROUGH NOAH, HUMANITY WOULD HAVE A SECOND CHANCE.
GOD WOULD NOT WIPE OUT EVERYONE. HE HAD A PLAN AND HIS MAN, RAINMAN.
MAKE YOURSELF AN ARK. AND I WILL MAKE A COVENANT WITH YOU. I PROMISE THAT I WILL SAVE YOU AND YOUR LOVED ONES FROM THE GREAT FLOOD I AM GOING TO SEND OVER THE EARTH.
WARNED BY GOD, RAINMAN, IN FAITH, BUILT AN ARK TO SAVE HIS FAMILY.
AND THE ANIMALS.
WHAT'S HE DOING?
CRAZY MAN!
THAT BOAT WON'T FLOAT.

WATERWORLD
SO RAINMAN BUILT HIS ARK.
AND INTO IT WENT PAIRS OF EVERY ANIMAL. AND THE EIGHT MEMBERS OF HIS FAMILY.
THEN THE RAIN CAME.
AND THE HEAVENS OPENED.
FOR 40 DAYS AND 40 NIGHTS IT RAINED.
A SUPER-STORM
AND ALL THE FLESH OF THE EARTH AND THE BIRDS OF THE AIR PERISHED IN THE WATERS.

RAINBOW MAN

THE WATER RECEDED FROM THE LAND.
RAINMAN SENT OUT A DOVE TO FIND DRY LAND. AFTER MANY DAYS, THE DOVE RETURNED WITH AN OLIVE BRANCH.
SEVEN DAYS LATER HE SENT IT OUT AGAIN. IT DIDN'T RETURN. RAINMAN COULD NOW LEAVE THE ARK.
AND GOD GAVE RAINMAN A SIGN IN THE HEAVENS, A PROMISE THAT NEVER AGAIN WOULD A FLOOD DESTROY ALL LIVING THINGS.
BE FRUITFUL AND MULTIPLY!
RAINMAN BECAME RAINBOW MAN.

DARK TOWER
OVER TIME THE EARTH BECAME POPULATED AGAIN. ONE PEOPLE AND ONE LANGUAGE.
THE GREAT HUNTER NIMROD BUILT A MEGA CITY ON THE PLAINS OF BABYLON.
IN THE MIDST OF THE CITY, A MIGHTY TOWER REACHED INTO THE HEAVENS.
THE TOWER WAS A SYMBOL OF THE PEOPLE'S ARROGANCE AND SELFISH AMBITION.
GOD WAS DISPLEASED WITH THEIR PRIDE.
SO HE CONFUSED THEM BY SPLINTERING THEIR ONE LANGUAGE INTO MANY.
THE CITY WAS THEREFORE NAMED BABEL, CONFUSION.
AND THE PEOPLE WERE SCATTERED THROUGHOUT THE EARTH.

FAITHMAN
CENTURIES PASSED...
ABRAM LIVED AMONG THE SCATTERED NATIONS OF THE EARTH IN HARAN.
GOD CALLED ABRAM TO LEAVE AND GO TO A NEW COUNTRY.
A NEW COUNTRY FOR AN OLD MAN.
FAITHMAN.
I WILL MAKE YOU THE FATHER OF A GREAT NATION.
I WILL BLESS YOU, SO THAT YOU WILL BE A BLESSING.
IN YOU, ALL PEOPLES OF THE EARTH SHALL BE BLESSED.
FAITHMAN GATHERED TOGETHER ALL HIS POSSESSIONS, AND SET OFF WITH SARAI, HIS WIFE, AND HIS NEPHEW LOT TOWARD THE LAND OF CANAAN. INTO THE UNKNOWN.

BUT THE JOURNEY WAS TRICKY.
FAITHMAN AND LOT HAD BOTH BROUGHT THEIR FLOCKS AND HERDS WITH THEM. BUT AS RESOURCES BECAME SCARCE, ARGUMENTS FLARED UP.
FAITHMAN AND LOT AGREED TO SEPARATE AND GO IN DIFFERENT DIRECTIONS.
THE LANDS AT THAT TIME WERE RULED BY MANY TRIBAL LEADERS WHOSE EGOS DROVE THEM TO WARS AND CONQUESTS.
LOT SETTLED IN SODOM, BUT WAS CAUGHT UP IN THE BATTLE OF THE NINE KINGS AND...
...TAKEN.
CAPTIVE!
FAITHMAN GOT THE NEWS.
COME QUICKLY!
FAITHMAN CAME TO THE RESCUE.
AGAINST ALL THE ODDS, HE OVERCAME LOT'S CAPTORS.
AND FAITHMAN AND LOT WERE REUNITED.
MELCHIZEDEK, THE PRIEST KING OF SALEM, **PEACEMAKER**, BLESSED FAITHMAN AFTER HIS VICTORY.
IN RETURN, FAITHMAN GAVE HIM A TENTH OF WHAT HE OWNED.

STARS IN HIS EYES
GOD PROMISED FAITHMAN DESCENDANTS AS NUMEROUS AS THE STARS.
DO NOT BE AFRAID. I AM YOUR SHIELD. YOUR REWARD WILL BE GREAT.
HOW WILL YOU BLESS ME, LORD? I HAVE NO CHILDREN.
LOOK AT THE STARS! YOU WILL HAVE AS MANY DESCENDANTS AS THERE ARE STARS.
FAITHMAN TRUSTED GOD, AND THIS WAS COUNTED TO HIM AS RIGHTEOUSNESS.

PARENTHOOD

BUT SARAI COULD NOT BELIEVE THAT SHE WOULD HAVE A CHILD. SHE WAS OLD.

SHE HAD HER OWN PLAN TO HELP GOD AND FAITHMAN.

SHE GAVE HAGAR, HER MAID, TO FAITHMAN AS A WIFE.

AND SOON ENOUGH...

...HAGAR CONCEIVED.

AND SHE GAVE BIRTH TO ISHMAEL.

OVER TEN YEARS LATER...
GOD CONFIRMED HIS COVENANT WITH FAITHMAN.
THREE ANGELS
YOU WILL BE NAMED ABRAHAM, FATHER OF MANY NATIONS.
SARAI WILL BE NAMED SARAH, AND SHE WILL HAVE A SON NAMED ISAAC.
AND I WILL BE YOUR GOD.
ONE DAY AT HIGH NOON...
THREE MYSTERY MEN APPROACHED FAITHMAN'S CAMP.
FAITHMAN GREETED THEM AND INVITED THEM IN TO LUNCH.
COME...YOU MUST EAT AND REST BEFORE YOU CONTINUE YOUR JOURNEY.
YOUR WIFE, SARAH, WILL HAVE A CHILD NEXT YEAR.
SARAH OVERHEARD.
AND LAUGHED.
SARAH WAS SUDDENLY AFRAID.
IS ANYTHING TOO HARD FOR THE LORD TO DO?
NOW WE MUST GO TO SODOM AND SEE WHAT THEY HAVE DONE.

SIN CITY
TWO OF THE ANGELS ARRIVED AT LOT'S HOUSE IN SODOM. HE WELCOMED THEM.
YOU MUST LEAVE THIS PLACE BECAUSE GOD WILL DESTROY IT TONIGHT.
THE MEN OF SODOM CAME TO LOT'S HOUSE.
BRING OUT THOSE MEN SO THAT WE CAN ABUSE THEM!
THIS IS WICKEDNESS! DON'T DO IT!
THE ANGELS BLINDED THE MOB TO PROTECT LOT'S FAMILY.
I CAN'T SEE!
AHH!
STOP TOUCHING ME. WHERE ARE THEY?
!
THE ANGELS DRAGGED LOT AND HIS FAMILY FROM THE CITY AS FIRE AND BRIMSTONE RAINED DOWN ON SODOM.
FLEE TO THE HILLS, LOT! AND DON'T STOP OR LOOK BACK!
BUT LOT'S WIFE DID NOT ESCAPE.
SHE DISOBEYED, BY LOOKING BACK, AND WAS TURNED INTO A PILLAR OF SALT.

THE FOLLOWING YEAR, AGAINST ALL THE ODDS, ISAAC WAS BORN.
WOW!
BECAUSE I LAUGHED AT THE LORD, HIS NAME SHALL BE **LAUGHTER**.

LAUGHTER
THEN GOD TESTED FAITHMAN.
SACRIFICE YOUR SON!
HOW CAN I DISOBEY GOD?

WHERE IS THE LAMB, FATHER?
GOD WILL PROVIDE THE LAMB, MY SON.

STOP! NOW I KNOW THAT THAT YOU HAVE FAITH.
FAITHMAN HAD PASSED THE TEST.

FAITHMAN THEN SPOTTED A RAM AND SACRIFICED IT INSTEAD.

I WILL BLESS YOU. AND BY YOUR OFFSPRING THE NATIONS OF THE WORLD WILL ALSO BE BLESSED.

LATER...
FAITHMAN SENT HIS SERVANT TO FIND LAUGHTER A BRIDE FROM HIS HOMELAND.
THE MATCHMAKER ARRIVED AT HARAN AND MET REBEKAH.
THROUGH HER KINDNESS, GOD SHOWED HIM THAT REBEKAH WAS THE ONE HE HAD CHOSEN.

REBEKAH'S FAMILY AGREED TO THE MARRIAGE.
AND THE MATCHMAKER RETURNED WITH REBEKAH.

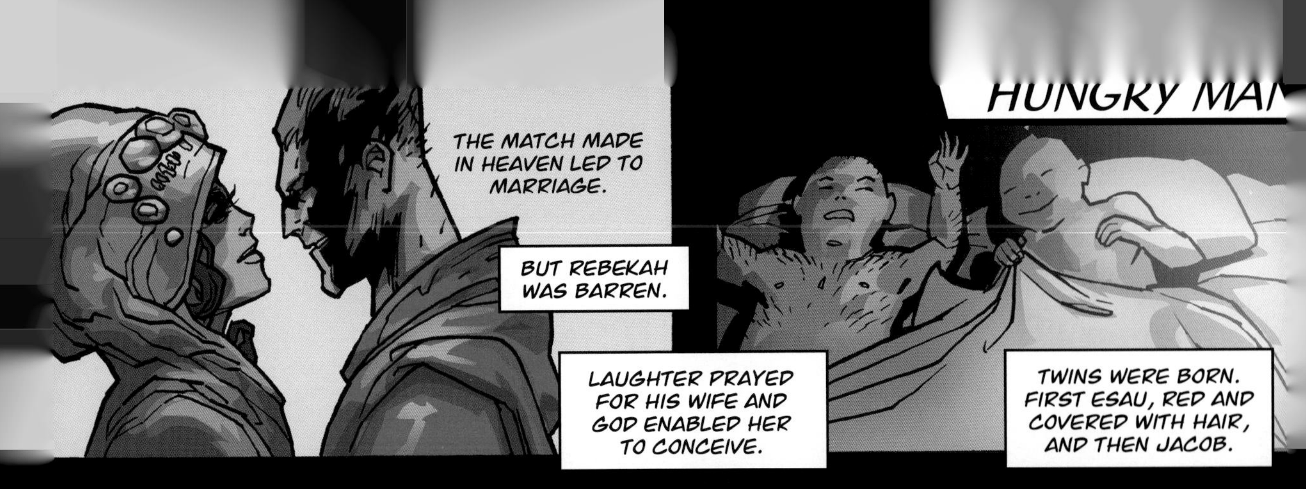
THE MATCH MADE IN HEAVEN LED TO MARRIAGE.
BUT REBEKAH WAS BARREN.
LAUGHTER PRAYED FOR HIS WIFE AND GOD ENABLED HER TO CONCEIVE.
TWINS WERE BORN. FIRST ESAU, RED AND COVERED WITH HAIR, AND THEN JACOB.

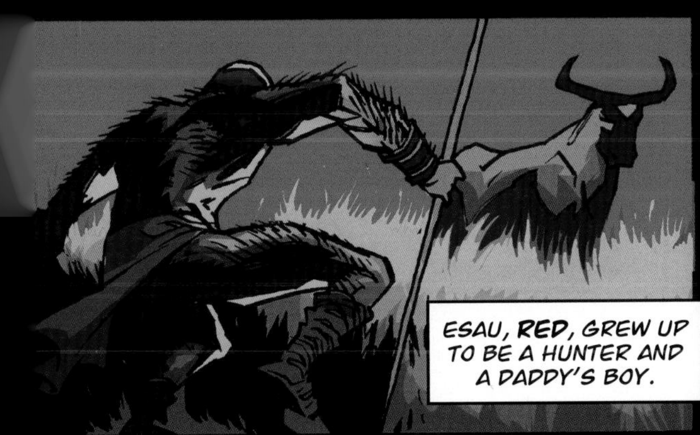
ESAU, **RED**, GREW UP TO BE A HUNTER AND A DADDY'S BOY.

WHILST JACOB, **CUNNING**, GREW UP TO BE A GREAT COOK AND HIS MOTHER'S FAVORITE.

ONE DAY AFTER A HUNT, RED CAME HOME HUNGRY.
WHAT ARE YOU COOKING?
RED STEW.
AH! THAT'S MY FAVORITE.

I'D GIVE MY RIGHT ARM FOR SOME OF THAT.
GIVE ME YOUR BIRTHRIGHT AND IT'S A DEAL.

DONE. WHAT GOOD IS A BIRTHRIGHT IF I DIE OF HUNGER?

CUNNING WAS LIVING UP TO HIS NAME.

LAUGHTER WAS OLD AND BLIND NOW, AND NEEDED TO PASS ON HIS BIRTHRIGHT BEFORE HE DIED.
RED! GO, MY SON, AND PREPARE ME A MEAL. THEN I WILL BLESS YOU.

BUT REBEKAH DID NOT WANT TO SEE HER FAVORITE SON CUNNING OUTDONE.

QUICKLY GO AND PREPARE! YOU MUST GET THE BIRTHRIGHT.

CUNNING DISGUISED HIMSELF AS THE MORE RUGGED RED.
HERE, FATHER. EAT.

YOU SOUND LIKE CUNNING BUT FEEL LIKE RED.
AND SO CUNNING RECEIVED THE BLESSING.

NOT LONG AFTER...
HERE, FATHER. EAT.

OH NO! RED! WE HAVE BEEN TRICKED! CUNNING HAS TAKEN YOUR BLESSING.
I'LL KILL HIM!

REALIZING THAT HER SON WAS IN DANGER, REBEKAH URGED CUNNING TO FLEE TO HER BROTHER IN HARAN TO LIE LOW.

STAR-GATE
CUNNING RAN UNTIL EVENING. BUT THEN HE WAS TIRED AND NEEDED TO REST.
THAT WILL MAKE A GOOD PILLOW.
BUT THIS WAS NO ORDINARY PLACE. AND CUNNING HAD NO ORDINARY DREAM...
WHAT?!
CUNNING SAW A STAIRWAY FROM EARTH TO HEAVEN.
OH!
I AM THE LORD AND I AM WITH YOU.
I WILL GIVE TO YOU AND YOUR OFFSPRING THIS LAND ON WHICH YOU LIE.
AND ALL PEOPLE WILL BE BLESSED THROUGH YOU.
WHEN CUNNING AWOKE, HE MADE AN ALTAR.
HE NAMED THE PLACE BETHEL, WHICH MEANS "HOUSE OF GOD".

CUNNING ARRIVED AT THE HOME OF HIS UNCLE LABAN.
WHAT A BEAUTIFUL GIRL!
THE TRICKSTERS
CUNNING WAS IN LOVE.
SO HE ASKED LABAN FOR HIS COUSIN'S HAND IN MARRIAGE.
I WANT TO MARRY RACHEL.
WORK FOR ME FOR SEVEN YEARS AND SHE'S YOURS.
BUT CUNNING HAD MET HIS MATCH IN HIS DEVIOUS UNCLE.
AFTER SEVEN YEARS, LABAN TRICKED CUNNING INTO MARRYING LEAH, HIS ELDEST DAUGHTER, INSTEAD OF RACHEL.
HOW CAN I MARRY OFF MY YOUNGER BEFORE MY ELDEST DAUGHTER? BUT I WILL GIVE YOU RACHEL IF YOU WORK FOR ME FOR ANOTHER SEVEN YEARS.
VERY WELL.
AND SO CUNNING HAD TWO WIVES, LEAH AND RACHEL.
AFTER SEVEN MORE YEARS OF WORK, CUNNING WANTED TO GO BACK HOME.
MY BIRTHRIGHT MEANS NOTHING HERE. I MUST RETURN TO THE LAND OF MY FATHER.
AS MY WAGES, LET ME TAKE FROM YOUR FLOCKS THE SPECKLED AND SPOTTED SHEEP AND GOATS, AND EVERY BLACK LAMB.
DEAL.
CUNNING FOUND A CLEVER WAY TO BREED STRONG LIVESTOCK THAT WERE SPECKLED OR SPOTTED.
THE STING WAS ON...
AFTER THE FIRST YEAR, CUNNING'S FLOCKS WERE GROWING FASTER AND WERE STRONGER THAN LABAN'S.
YOU HAVE LEFT ME WITH ALL THE WEAK ANIMALS, YOU THIEF! I HAVE BEEN TRICKED!
CUNNING WAS ON THE RUN AGAIN.
HURRY! WE MUST GO. IT'S TIME TO CLAIM MY BIRTHRIGHT.

FIGHT NIGHT
CUNNING AND HIS FAMILY HEADED FOR HIS HOMELAND.
AFRAID OF HIS BROTHER RED'S MOOD TOWARD HIM, CUNNING DIVIDED HIS FAMILY INTO TWO GROUPS, AND SENT FLOCKS AND CATTLE AHEAD AS GIFTS.
O GOD, PLEASE PROTECT ME!
THAT NIGHT CUNNING WAS AWAKENED.
A STRANGE FIGURE APPEARED.
AND THE RESTLESS NIGHT TURNED INTO A WRESTLING MATCH.
ON ONE SIDE, CUNNING.
ON THE OTHER, THE ULTIMATE FIGHTER.
I WILL NOT LET YOU GO UNLESS YOU BLESS ME.
SO JACOB, THE CUNNING MAN, WAS RENAMED ISRAEL, THE CONTENDER.
FROM NOW ON YOU WILL BE CALLED ISRAEL...THE ONE WHO CONTENDS WITH GOD AND WITH PEOPLE, FOR YOU HAVE PREVAILED.

DREAMBOY
BETWEEN HIS TWO WIVES AND THEIR MAIDS, THE CONTENDER HAD TWELVE CHILDREN. BUT HIS FAVORITES WERE THE CHILDREN OF RACHEL: JOSEPH, DREAMBOY, AND BENJAMIN.
DREAMBOY WAS GIVEN A ROBE OF MANY COLORS, A CLOAK OF HONOR BY HIS FATHER.
I DREAMED THAT THE SUN AND THE MOON AND ELEVEN STARS WERE BOWING DOWN TO ME.
HIS BROTHERS WERE NOT HAPPY.
JEALOUSY SET IN.
WHACK!
THUMP!
THEY PLOTTED.
LET'S NOT KILL HIM BUT THROW HIM INTO THIS PIT.
WHILE THEY WERE ARGUING OVER WHAT TO DO, A BAND OF SLAVE TRADERS WAS PASSING BY.
A DECISION WAS MADE. DREAMBOY WAS HANDED OVER IN RETURN FOR TWENTY PIECES OF SILVER.

FATAL ATTRACTION
IN EGYPT, DREAMBOY WAS SOLD...
...TO POTIPHAR, ONE OF PHARAOH'S OFFICIALS. THE CAPTAIN OF THE GUARD.
THERE DREAMBOY EXCELLED IN ALL HIS DUTIES, AS GOD WAS WITH HIM.
BUT...
...DREAMBOY SOON CAUGHT THE EYE OF POTIPHAR'S WIFE.
HE RESISTED THE ADVANCES OF THE FEMME FATALE.
HE TRIED TO SLEEP WITH ME!
A WOMAN SCORNED. SHE WANTED REVENGE.
POTIPHAR BURNED WITH ANGER AND HAD DREAMBOY THROWN INTO PRISON.
DREAMBOY FEARED THAT HIS DREAMS WOULD NEVER COME TRUE. BUT GOD WAS WITH HIM.

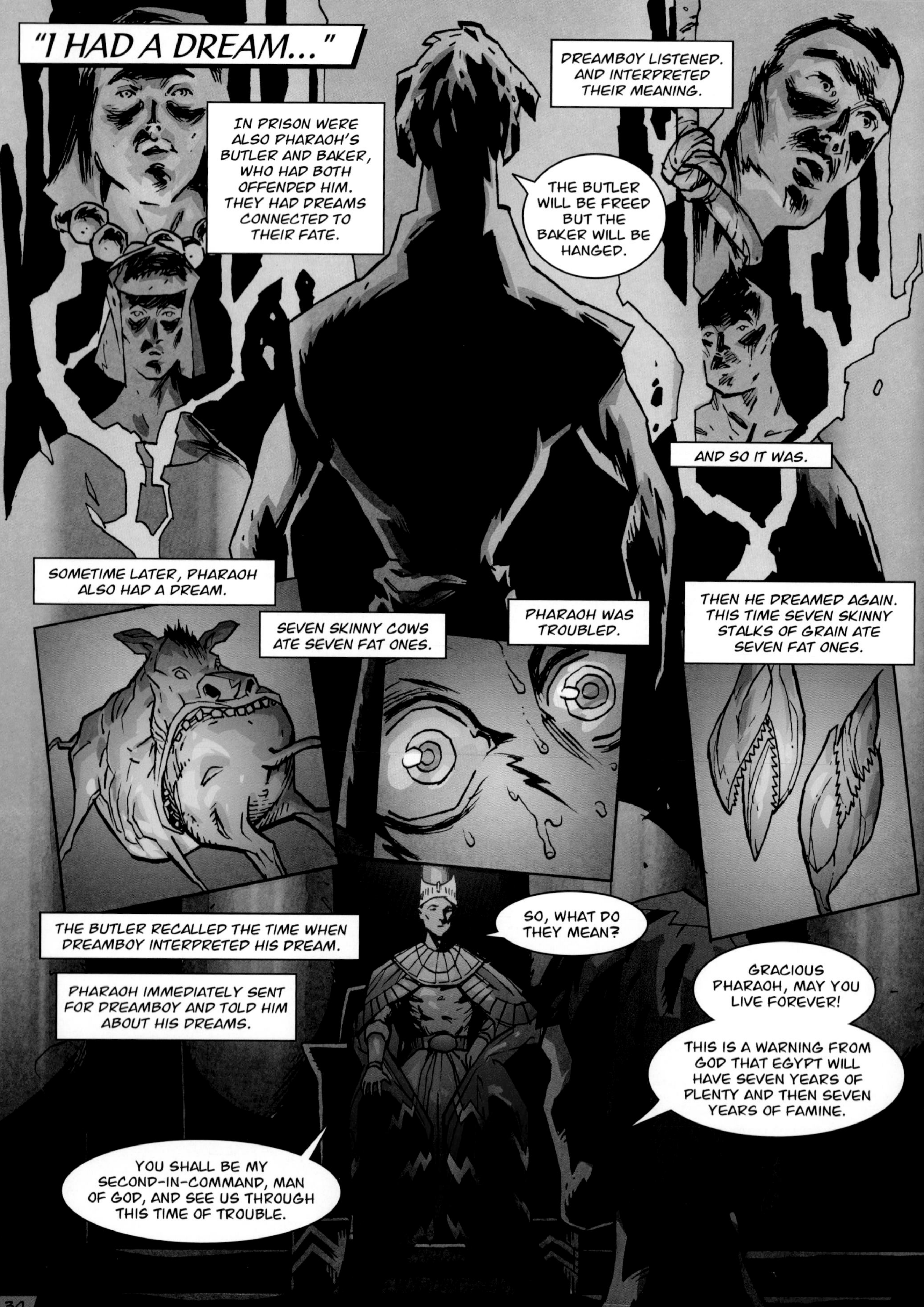

"I HAD A DREAM..."
IN PRISON WERE ALSO PHARAOH'S BUTLER AND BAKER, WHO HAD BOTH OFFENDED HIM. THEY HAD DREAMS CONNECTED TO THEIR FATE.
DREAMBOY LISTENED. AND INTERPRETED THEIR MEANING.
THE BUTLER WILL BE FREED BUT THE BAKER WILL BE HANGED.
AND SO IT WAS.
SOMETIME LATER, PHARAOH ALSO HAD A DREAM.
SEVEN SKINNY COWS ATE SEVEN FAT ONES.
PHARAOH WAS TROUBLED.
THEN HE DREAMED AGAIN. THIS TIME SEVEN SKINNY STALKS OF GRAIN ATE SEVEN FAT ONES.
THE BUTLER RECALLED THE TIME WHEN DREAMBOY INTERPRETED HIS DREAM.
PHARAOH IMMEDIATELY SENT FOR DREAMBOY AND TOLD HIM ABOUT HIS DREAMS.
SO, WHAT DO THEY MEAN?
GRACIOUS PHARAOH, MAY YOU LIVE FOREVER!
THIS IS A WARNING FROM GOD THAT EGYPT WILL HAVE SEVEN YEARS OF PLENTY AND THEN SEVEN YEARS OF FAMINE.
YOU SHALL BE MY SECOND-IN-COMMAND, MAN OF GOD, AND SEE US THROUGH THIS TIME OF TROUBLE.

BY STORING GRAIN DURING THE YEARS OF PLENTY, DREAMBOY ENSURED THAT FOR EGYPT FEAST WOULD NOT TURN INTO FAMINE.
BUT AFTER SEVEN YEARS, FAMINE SPREAD THROUGH EVERY OTHER COUNTRY.
THE CONTENDER HEARD THAT THERE WAS STILL FOOD IN EGYPT AND TOLD HIS SONS TO GO THERE.
AND SO DREAMBOY'S BROTHERS MADE THE LONG JOURNEY.
WHEN THEY ARRIVED, DREAMBOY RECOGNIZED HIS BROTHERS, BUT THEY DID NOT RECOGNIZE HIM.
DREAMBOY DECIDED TO TEST THEM BY HAVING HIS SILVER CUP SLIPPED INTO THE GRAIN HE GAVE THEM.
STOP AND SEARCH!
BENJAMIN WAS FOUND WITH THE CUP.
DON'T PUNISH BENJAMIN. PUNISH ME!
DREAMBOY KNEW THAT HIS BROTHERS WERE CHANGED MEN.
I AM YOUR BROTHER! DON'T BE AFRAID. YOU MEANT TO HARM ME, BUT GOD TURNED IT TO GOOD.
DREAMBOY INSTRUCTED THEM TO BRING HIS FATHER AND THE REST OF THEIR FAMILY TO EGYPT.
RECONCILED.

DEATH ON THE NILE
LONG AFTER THE MEMORY OF DREAMBOY'S ACCOMPLISHMENTS HAD FADED, A NEW PHARAOH CAME TO POWER. THREATENED BY THE NUMBER OF ISRAELITES, HE PERSECUTED THEM, AND MADE THEM INTO SLAVES.
THE CHILDREN OF ISRAEL MULTIPLIED GREATLY IN THE LAND OF EGYPT AS GOD HAD PROMISED.
IF IT IS A BOY, KILL IT!
WHEN THEIR POPULATION CONTINUED TO INCREASE, PHARAOH ORDERED THE MIDWIVES TO KILL THE MALE BABIES.
FEARING GOD, THEY DEFIED PHARAOH AND KEPT THE BABIES ALIVE.
SO PHARAOH ISSUED A NEW COMMAND. ALL MALE ISRAELITE BABIES WERE TO BE DROWNED IN THE NILE.
DETERMINED NOT TO SEE HER GOLDEN CHILD DIE, ONE MOTHER HID HER SON IN A BASKET ON THE RIVER.
GOD, I GIVE OUR SON TO YOU. WATCH OVER HIM AND KEEP HIM SAFE.

THE RIVER BABY

HOLY FIRE
WOW!
THAT'S STRANGE! WHY DOES THAT BUSH NOT BURN UP?
WATERMAN! THIS IS HOLY GROUND.
I HAVE SEEN THE MISERY OF MY PEOPLE. I HAVE COME TO RESCUE THEM.
I AM WHO I AM IS SENDING YOU BACK.
HOW CAN I GO BACK? I AM A WANTED MAN, AND I CANNOT SPEAK WELL.
DO NOT FEAR, BECAUSE I AM WITH YOU.
GOD GOES NINE ROUNDS WITH EGYPT.
ROUND 1: BLOOD IN THE NILE
ROUND 2: FROGS
ROUND 3: GNATS
ROUND 4: FLIES
ROUND 5: DEAD LIVESTOCK
ROUND 6: BOILS
LET GOD'S PEOPLE GO, PHARAOH!
WHO IS GOD THAT I SHOULD OBEY HIS VOICE?
THE WORDS OF WATERMAN FELL ON THE CLOSED EARS OF PHARAOH, SO GOD BEGAN TO JUDGE THE EGYPTIAN NATION, SENDING PLAGUES UPON THEM.

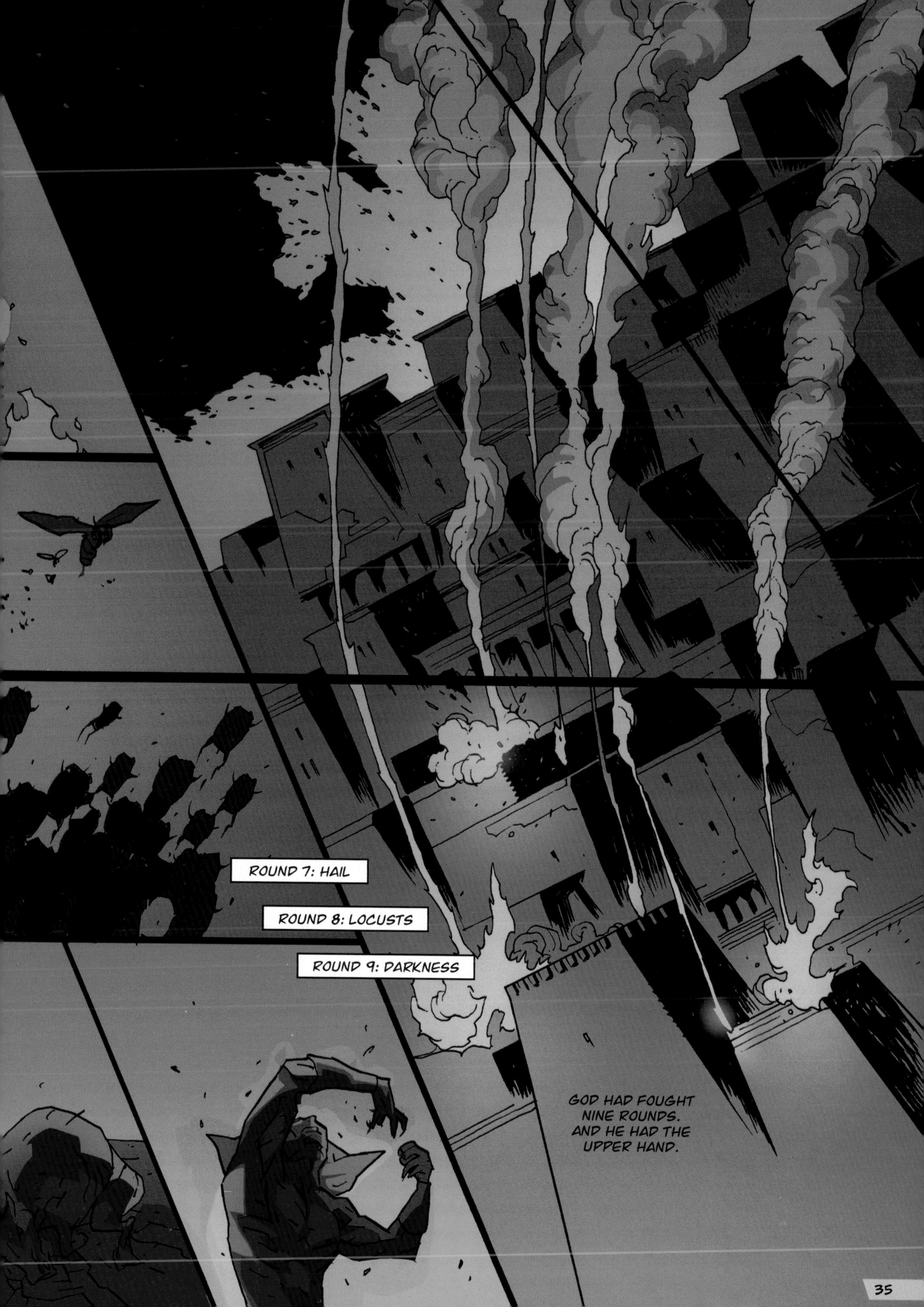
ROUND 7: HAIL
ROUND 8: LOCUSTS
ROUND 9: DARKNESS
GOD HAD FOUGHT NINE ROUNDS. AND HE HAD THE UPPER HAND.

PASSOVER NIGHT

THE GRIEF AT THE LOSS IN EACH HOME WAS TOO MUCH TO BEAR.
GO!
THIS FINAL ROUND WAS A KNOCK-OUT BLOW, WITH THE DEATH OF PHARAOH'S OWN FIRSTBORN. PHARAOH GAVE IN.
THAT NIGHT THE ISRAELITES URGENTLY PREPARED TO LEAVE EGYPT, AND BY MORNING WERE ON THEIR WAY.
WE LOST THE FIGHT. BUT WE ARE FREE OF THE ISRAELITES AND THEIR GOD.

BUT PHARAOH'S PRIDE GOT THE BETTER OF HIS GRIEF.
I WILL NOT LOSE A FIGHT TO SLAVES. KILL THEM ALL!
PHARAOH ASSEMBLED HIS ARMY AND CHARIOTS TO GO IN PURSUIT OF THE ISRAELITES.
YAH!
BUT THE ISRAELITES WERE UNDER THE PROTECTION OF GOD. HE SHOWED THEM WHERE TO GO WITH A PILLAR OF CLOUD BY DAY AND A PILLAR OF FIRE BY NIGHT.

THE EGYPTIANS BELIEVED THAT THEY HAD THE ISRAELITES TRAPPED BY THE RED SEA. BUT WATERMAN STRETCHED OUT HIS HAND OVER THE WATER, AND GOD SENT A MIGHTY WIND TO CREATE A PATH THROUGH THE WAVES.
BEHOLD THE GREAT POWER OF THE LORD!
TRUSTING IN GOD, THE ISRAELITES PASSED ACROSS THE RED SEA AS IF IT WERE DRY LAND.
AS THE LAST ISRAELITE STEPPED ON TO THE OTHER SIDE, WATERMAN STRETCHED HIS HAND OUT AGAIN, AND THE WAVES CLOSED IN. ALL THE EGYPTIANS PURSUING THEM WERE DROWNED.
ISRAEL WAS FREE.

INTO THE WILDERNESS

THE WILDERNESS BECAME A GRAVEYARD FOR MANY.
WHEN THE ISRAELITES REACHED MOUNT SINAI, WATERMAN WENT UP THE HOLY MOUNTAIN. AND GOD CAME TO HIM IN A CLOUD.
I AM THE LORD YOUR GOD, WHO BROUGHT YOU OUT OF EGYPT.
IF YOU OBEY MY COMMANDS AND KEEP MY COVENANT, YOU WILL BE A KINGDOM OF PRIESTS AND A HOLY NATION.
THE MOUNTAIN BURNED AS THE PRESENCE OF GOD DESCENDED.
THE ISRAELITES TREMBLED.
KEEP THE TEN COMMANDMENTS I HAVE GIVEN YOU SO THAT IT MAY GO WELL WITH YOU.
WATERMAN RETURNED FROM THE MOUNTAIN SHINING FROM THE GLORY OF GOD'S PRESENCE...NOW THE **LAW MAN** OF ISRAEL.
HEAR, O ISRAEL! THE LORD OUR GOD IS ONE LORD. LOVE THE LORD WITH ALL YOUR HEART, SOUL, AND STRENGTH.

VISION FOR A NATION

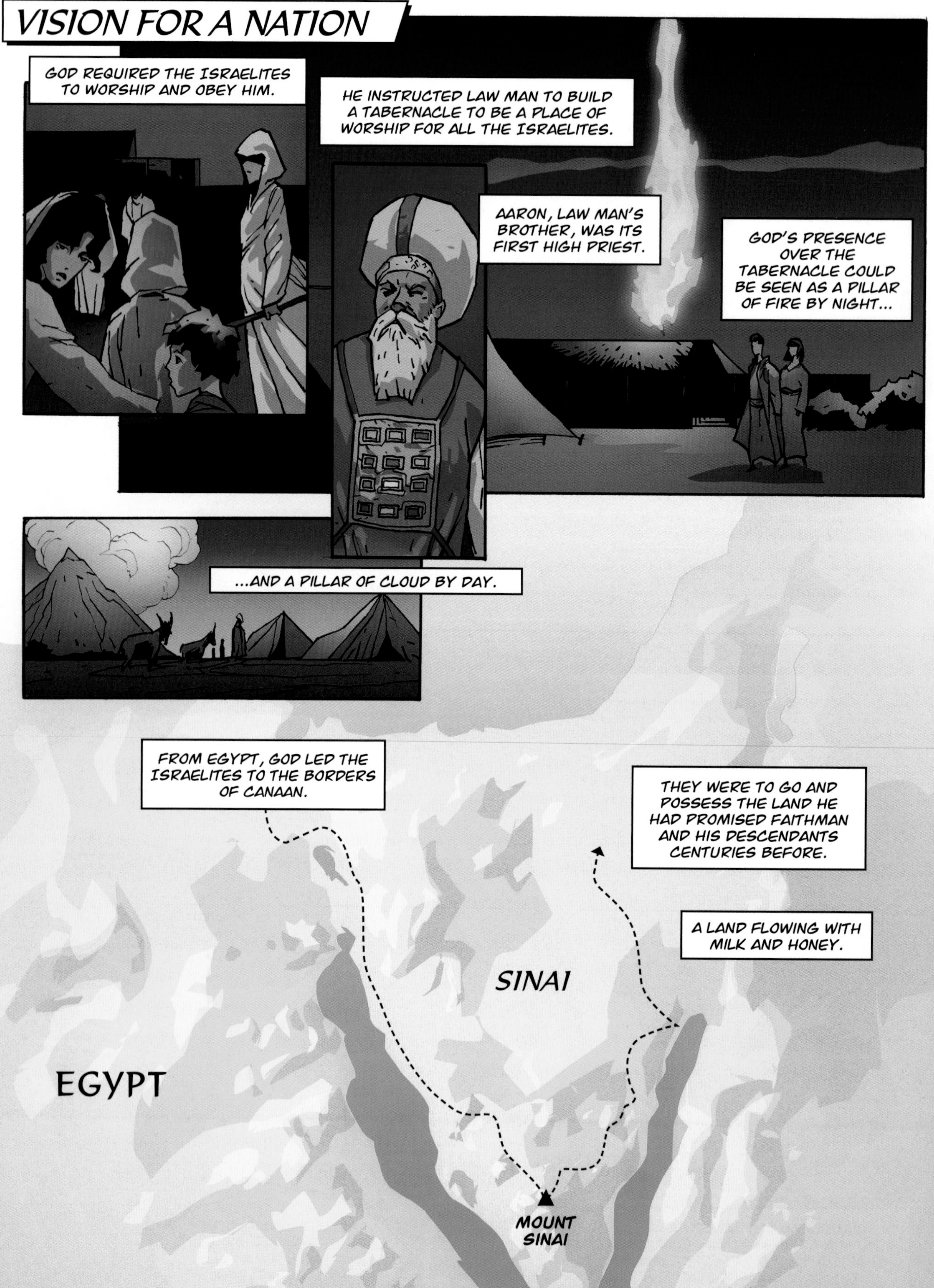

THE TABERNACLE WAS PLACED IN THE CENTRE OF THE CAMP, WITH THE ARK OF THE COVENANT CONTAINING THE TEN COMMANDMENTS IN ITS MIDST.
LAW MAN SPOKE TO THE PEOPLE...
BRING YOUR SACRIFICES TO THE TABERNACLE TO WORSHIP GOD AND TO ATONE FOR YOUR SINS.
BEFORE YOU IS LIFE AND PROSPERITY, DEATH AND DESTRUCTION.
LOVE THE LORD AND KEEP HIS COMMANDS.
CHOOSE LIFE! THEN THE LORD WILL BLESS YOU IN THE PROMISED LAND.

MISSION: IMPOSSIBLE

THE LAND OF CANAAN WAS POPULATED BY MANY PAGAN AND CRUEL NATIONS THAT LIVED IN FORTIFIED CITIES. GIANTS WERE ALSO REPORTED TO LIVE THERE.

TAKING THIS LAND WILL BE A CHALLENGE, FOR SURE.
LOOK AT THE SIZE OF THOSE GRAPES!
ON THEIR RETURN, THEY BROUGHT MANY OF THE FRUITS OF THE LAND.
WOW! THE LAND IS TRULY BLESSED.
THIS IS TOO GOOD TO BE TRUE.
THE LAND IS GOOD BUT WE CANNOT DEFEAT THESE NATIONS.
THIS IS MISSION IMPOSSIBLE.
HAVE YOU BROUGHT US HERE TO DIE?
WE WERE BETTER OFF IN EGYPT.
WE SHOULD GO BACK!
JOSHUA AND I THINK WE CAN BEAT THEM! WITH GOD, NOTHING IS IMPOSSIBLE.
CALEB IS RIGHT, WE HAVE SEEN GOD DO GREAT THINGS. THIS WILL BE NO DIFFERENT.
GOD IS NOT PLEASED WITH YOUR LACK OF FAITH.
YOU HAVE TREATED GOD WITH CONTEMPT! NONE OF YOU WILL ENTER THE PROMISED LAND APART FROM CALEB AND JOSHUA.

40 YEARS OF WANDERING

BUT THE TALLER THEY ARE...
I WILL KILL YOU, LAW MAN.
THE HARDER...
LORD, GUIDE MY SPEAR!
...THEY FALL.
AARGH!

IN SIGHT OF THE PROMISED LAND

SUFFERING MAN
IN THE LAND OF UZ, THERE LIVED A MAN CALLED JOB...
JOB HAD IT ALL.
FAMILY.
WEALTH.
AND HEALTH.
BUT SATAN, THE ACCUSER, ASKED GOD TO TEST JOB, AND IN THE SPACE OF ONE DAY IT WAS ALL GONE.
BY EVENING, IN HIS HUMBLED STATE, JOB, SUFFERING MAN, FOUND NO SOLACE.
THE SCOURGING TONGUES OF HIS WIFE AND FRIENDS CONTINUED TO LASH AGAINST HIS HOPE...
...AND HIS ENDURING FAITH IN HIS CREATOR.
CURSE GOD AND DIE!
YOU MUST HAVE DONE SOMETHING REALLY BAD!
BUT IN SPITE OF HIS PAIN, AND HIS QUESTIONING, SUFFERING MAN WAS NOT FOUND WANTING.
AND GOD BLESSED HIM.
TWICE OVER.

THE DELIVERER

THE SCARLET WOMAN

JERICHO AT NIGHT

WE MUST NOT DRAW ANY ATTENTION.

LOOK, THERE'S AN ENTRANCE.

THE RED-LIGHT DISTRICT

CAN WE LODGE HERE TONIGHT?

YOU ARE ISRAELITES! COME IN... QUICKLY.

THE PEOPLE OF THIS CITY FEAR YOU.

WE HAVE HEARD ABOUT THE DEFEAT OF OG AND THE EGYPTIANS...YOU ARE PROTECTED BY A MIGHTY GOD.

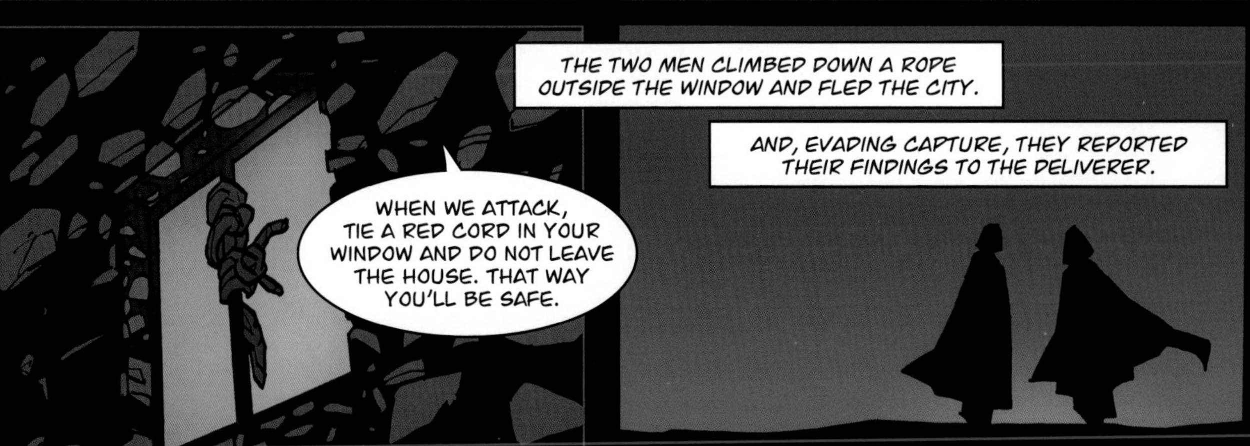

CROSSING THE JORDAN

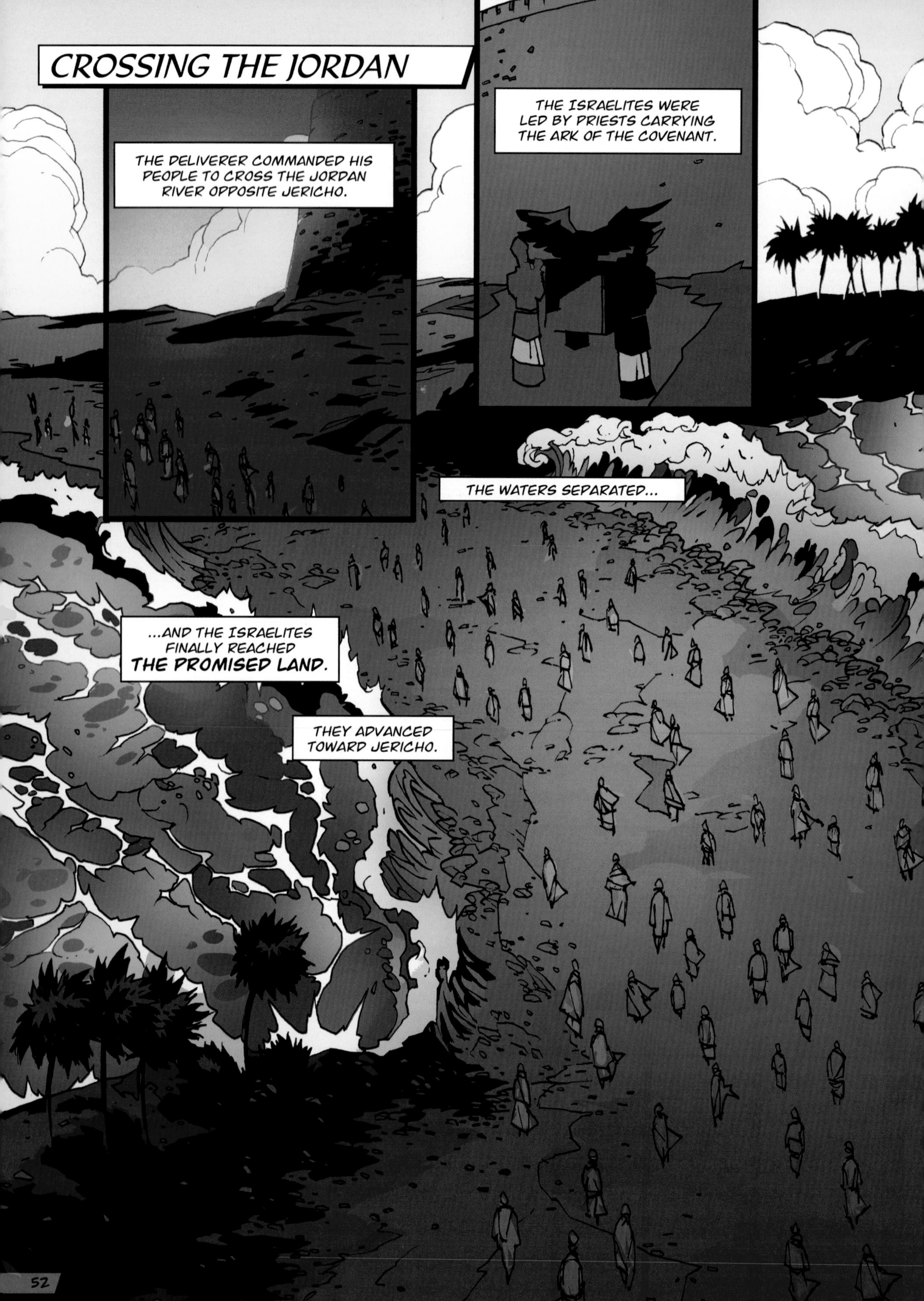

JUST OUTSIDE JERICHO, THE DELIVERER SAW A MAN IN FRONT OF HIM.
ARE YOU FOR US OR AGAINST US?
I SERVE THE LORD AND LEAD HIS ARMY.
WHAT MESSAGE DOES THE LORD HAVE FOR ME?
TAKE OFF YOUR SANDALS, FOR THIS IS HOLY GROUND.
THE DELIVERER OBEYED.

UNDER SIEGE
THE ISRAELITES MARCHED AROUND THE CITY WITHOUT SAYING A WORD. AND AGAIN ON THE SECOND DAY. EVERY DAY FOR SIX DAYS.
SOME PRIESTS CARRIED THE ARK OF THE COVENANT.
WHILE OTHERS SOUNDED THEIR TRUMPETS.
ON THE SEVENTH DAY, THE ISRAELITES MARCHED AROUND THE CITY SEVEN TIMES.
THE DELIVERER GAVE A MESSAGE TO HIS PEOPLE.
SHOUT OUT! THE LORD HAS GIVEN US THE CITY!
AND THE ISRAELITES GAVE A VICTORY SHOUT TO THE LORD THEIR GOD.

CRAAASH!
CRACK...
THE INHABITANTS WERE TERRIFIED.
AND THE CITY WALLS COLLAPSED.
ATTACK!

RUMBLE...
THE ISRAELITES OVERRAN THE CITY.
NOTHING WAS SPARED. NEITHER MAN, WOMAN, NOR ANIMAL.
EVERYTHING WAS BURNED TO THE GROUND.
ONLY SCARLET WOMAN AND HER HOUSEHOLD WERE SAVED FROM THE DESTRUCTION.

INVADED
THE ISRAELITE INVASION CONTINUED. THE AMORITE KINGS FROM THE HILL COUNTRIES MADE A DEFENCE PACT.
PIRAM OF JARMUTH
HOHAM OF HEBRON
ADONI-ZEDEK OF JERUSALEM
JAPHIA OF LACHISH
DEBIR OF EGLON
THESE ISRAELITES HAVE CONQUERED JERICHO AND AI.
THE POWERFUL CITY OF GIBEON HAS MADE A TREACHEROUS ALLIANCE WITH THEM.
WE MUST COME TOGETHER TO REPEL THEM.
HAVING AMASSED THEIR ARMIES, THEY SET OFF TO DEFEAT THE GIBEONITES.

THE LONGEST DAY

ASSEMBLE THE ARMY!

THE ISRAELITES SET OUT ON AN ALL-NIGHT MARCH TOWARD GIBEON...

...AND IN THE MORNING, TOOK THE AMORITES BY SURPRISE.

DON'T BE AFRAID! I WILL GIVE YOU VICTORY OVER THEM TODAY.
THEY ATTACKED THE AMORITE KINGS AT GIBEON...
...AND GOD KEPT THE SUN IN THE SKY UNTIL VICTORY WAS THEIRS.
THERE HAS NEVER BEEN SUCH A LONG DAY BEFORE IT OR SINCE.

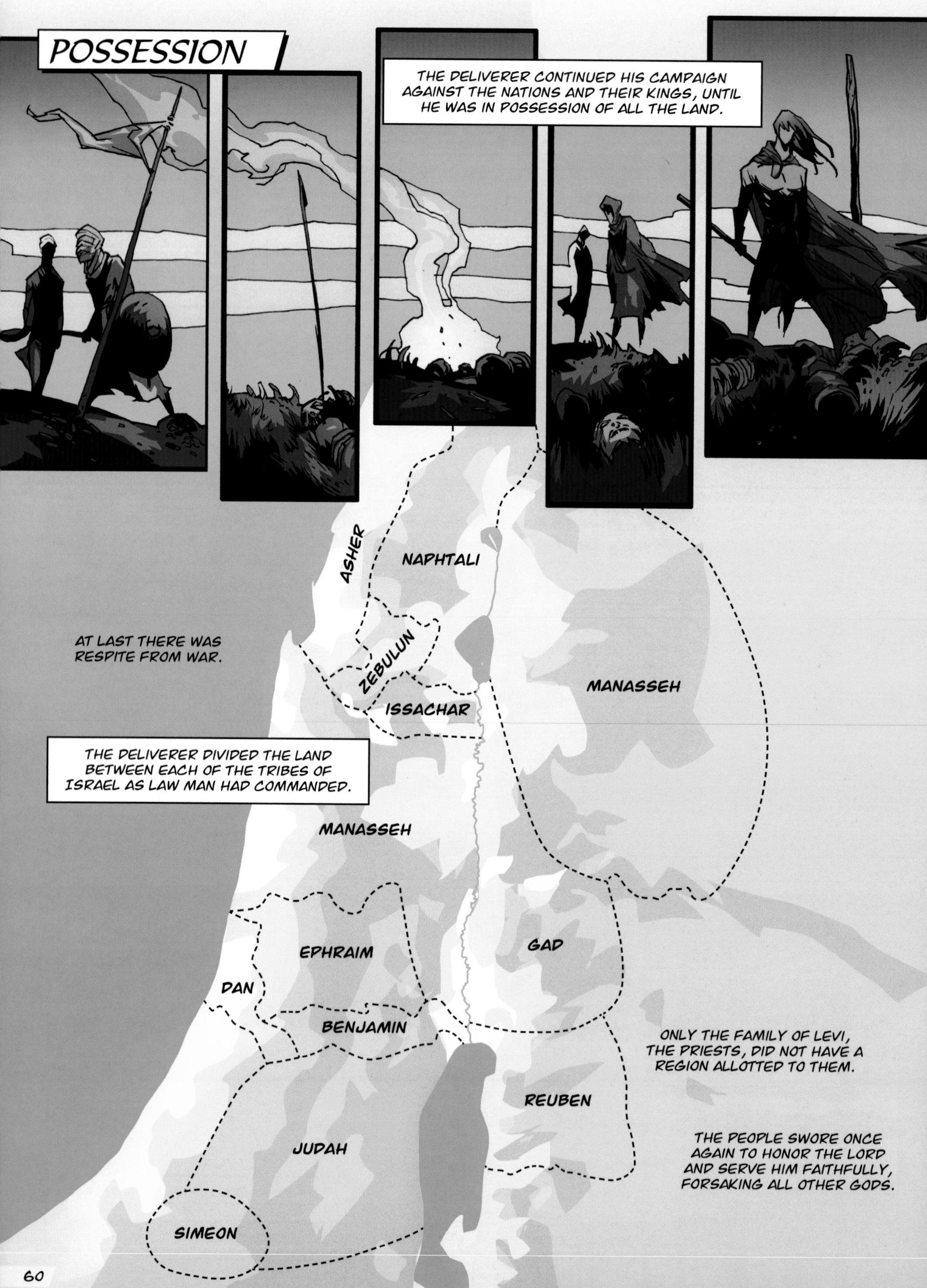
POSSESSION
THE DELIVERER CONTINUED HIS CAMPAIGN AGAINST THE NATIONS AND THEIR KINGS, UNTIL HE WAS IN POSSESSION OF ALL THE LAND.
AT LAST THERE WAS RESPITE FROM WAR.
THE DELIVERER DIVIDED THE LAND BETWEEN EACH OF THE TRIBES OF ISRAEL AS LAW MAN HAD COMMANDED.
ASHER
NAPHTALI
ZEBULUN
ISSACHAR
MANASSEH
MANASSEH
EPHRAIM
GAD
DAN
BENJAMIN
REUBEN
JUDAH
SIMEON
ONLY THE FAMILY OF LEVI, THE PRIESTS, DID NOT HAVE A REGION ALLOTTED TO THEM.
THE PEOPLE SWORE ONCE AGAIN TO HONOR THE LORD AND SERVE HIM FAITHFULLY, FORSAKING ALL OTHER GODS.

THE JUDGES' LEAGUE
THE DELIVERER AND HIS GENERATION DIED, AND A NEW GENERATION WAS BORN.
THE PEOPLE FORGOT THEIR ALLEGIANCE TO THE LORD, AND SERVED OTHER GODS.
יהוה
WITHOUT THE LORD'S BLESSING, THEY COULD NOT RESIST THE ENEMIES AROUND THEM.
SO GOD EMPOWERED WARRIOR JUDGES TO RESCUE ISRAEL, ONE AFTER ANOTHER.
THE FIRST THREE WERE:
OTHNIEL
EHUD
SHAMGAR
BUT AS EACH JUDGE DIED, THE PEOPLE WENT BACK TO THEIR BAD OLD WAYS.

THE PROPHETESS DEBORAH, THE IRON MAIDEN, WAS ALSO A JUDGE.
SHE LED THE ARMIES OF ZEBULUN AND NAPHTALI AGAINST SISERA THE CANAANITE AND HIS 900 IRON CHARIOTS.
SISERA ESCAPED, BUT JAEL, IRON MAIDEN #2, FINISHED HIM OFF WITH A METAL TENT PEG.
THE PEOPLE OF ISRAEL CONTINUED TO DISPLEASE THE LORD AND WORSHIP OTHER GODS.
MIDIANITES AND PEOPLES FROM THE EAST INVADED THE LAND.
EVERY HARVEST, THEY DESCENDED LIKE LOCUSTS AND RAVAGED THE ISRAELITES' LAND AND CROPS.
ENSLAVED AGAIN, ISRAEL CALLED OUT TO THE LORD.
ONE DAY A YOUNG MAN NAMED GIDEON WAS THRESHING WHEAT IN A WINE PRESS TO HIDE IT FROM THE MIDIANITES.
THE LORD IS WITH YOU, MIGHTY WARRIOR.
ME? I AM THE WEAKEST OF THE WEAK!
THE LORD IS SENDING YOU TO SAVE ISRAEL FROM MIDIAN.
GIVE ME A SIGN THAT THE LORD WANTS ME TO DO THIS...
...BY ACCEPTING THE SACRIFICE I BRING.
PUT YOUR OFFERING ON THIS ROCK.
SUDDENLY FIRE CONSUMED IT.
SURELY I HAVE SEEN THE ANGEL OF THE LORD!

MIGHTY WARRIOR CAMPAIGNED AGAINST THE LOCAL GODS AND THEIR WORSHIPERS.
BUT HE NEEDED MORE ASSURANCE.
LORD, IF YOU ARE WITH ME, TOMORROW LET THIS FLEECE BE WET AND THE GROUND DRY.
AND IT WAS AS HE HAD ASKED.
ONE MORE REQUEST. TOMORROW LET THE FLEECE BE DRY AND THE GROUND WET.
AND IT WAS AS HE HAD ASKED. NOW HE KNEW THE LORD WAS WITH HIM.
MIGHTY WARRIOR HAD 32,000 MEN.
BUT THE LORD SAID HE ONLY NEEDED 300.
COURAGE!
WITH JUST 300 MEN, MIGHTY WARRIOR SCARED THE MIDIANITES INTO FLIGHT.
THE MEN OF THE ISRAELITE TRIBE OF EPHRAIM ROSE UP, OVERCAME THE MIDIANITES, AND DROVE THEM FROM THE LAND.
BUT THE PEACE MIGHTY WARRIOR WON DID NOT LAST.
NOR DID ISRAEL'S FAITHFULNESS TO HER GOD.
MORE JUDGES CAME AND WENT. TOLA, JAIR, JEPHTHAH, AND OTHERS.
THERE WAS NO KING OVER ISRAEL. EVERYONE JUST DID WHAT THEY THOUGHT WAS RIGHT.

JUDGE DREADLOCKS

LATER...

THE PHILISTINES GOT THEIR CLAWS INTO THE ISRAELITES.

SAMSON

SET APART TO SERVE GOD.

INSTRUCTED NOT TO CUT HIS HAIR...

...JUDGE DREADLOCKS!

FELL FOR A PHILISTINE.

WENT TO MEET HER...

...LION ATTACK!

KABOOM!

THE SPIRIT OF THE LORD CAME ON DREADLOCKS AND HE TORE THE LION APART. HE TOLD HIS FAMILY HE HAD DECIDED TO MARRY THE PHILISTINE WOMAN...TO THEIR HORROR!

LATER, ON HIS WAY TO THE WEDDING
THAT'S STRANGE! BEES AND HONEY!

INSPIRED BY THE LION, DREADLOCKS POSED A RIDDLE AS A WAGER TO HIS WEDDING GUESTS.
OUT OF THE EATER CAME SOMETHING TO EAT, AND OUT OF THE MIGHTY CAME SOMETHING SWEET. 30 SHIRTS TO THE ONE WHO GETS THE ANSWER.
BEFORE THE DAYS OF FEASTING ARE OVER, WE WILL ANSWER YOUR RIDDLE.
STUMPED!

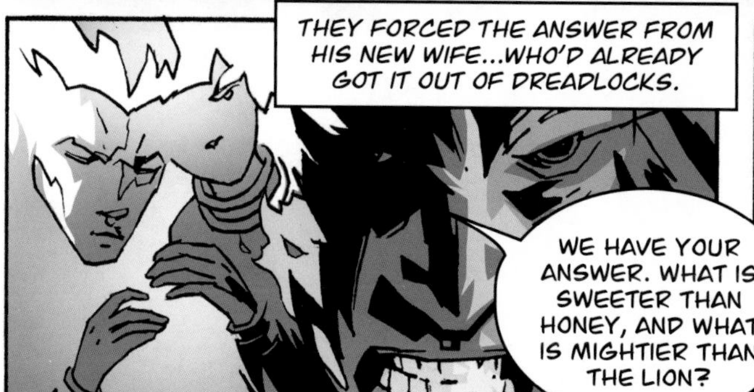
THEY FORCED THE ANSWER FROM HIS NEW WIFE...WHO'D ALREADY GOT IT OUT OF DREADLOCKS.
WE HAVE YOUR ANSWER. WHAT IS SWEETER THAN HONEY, AND WHAT IS MIGHTIER THAN THE LION?

THE PHILISTINE CITY OF ASHKELON
DREADLOCKS WAS **FURIOUS**.
I'LL SHOW THEM.

PAYBACK TIME.
DREADLOCKS SLAYED 30 PHILISTINE MEN...

...AND TOOK THEIR CLOTHES TO PAY THE DEBT HE OWED HIS GUESTS.
THEN HE RETURNED HOME, MINUS WIFE!

THINKING DREADLOCKS HAD ABANDONED HIS WIFE, THE PHILISTINES GAVE HER TO ANOTHER.
WHEN DREADLOCKS HEARD THIS, HE WAS FURIOUS. SO HE CAUGHT 300 FOXES, TIED THEIR TAILS...
...AND SET FIRE TO THEM IN THE FIELDS. ALL THE PHILISTINES' CROPS BURNED.
I WILL SHOW YOU THE MEANING OF ISRAELITE JUSTICE.
IN REVENGE, THE PHILISTINES KILLED HIS WIFE, AND TRIED TO ARREST HIM.
DREADLOCKS SLAYED 1,000 MEN WITH THE JAW OF A DONKEY.
LATER, TRAPPING HIM IN THE CITY OF GAZA, THE PHILISTINES TRIED TO CAPTURE HIM...AGAIN.
AARGH!
BUT DREADLOCKS MERELY LIFTED THE CITY GATES OFF THEIR HINGES AND CARRIED THEM AWAY.

DANGEROUS LIAISONS
ENTER DELILAH, AGENT PROVOCATEUR...
UNDERCOVER FOR THE PHILISTINES, AGENT PROVOCATEUR WAS ON A MISSION TO DISCOVER THE SECRET TO DREADLOCKS' MIRACULOUS STRENGTH.

DREADLOCKS WAS ENRAPTURED BY HER BEAUTY.
WOW!

BUT HE DID NOT SEE THAT HE WAS BEING BAITED.
YOU ARE SO STRONG, DREADLOCKS.

THE TRAP WAS SET.
WHAT IS THE SECRET OF YOUR STRENGTH?

IF YOU TIE ME WITH NEW ROPE, I WILL BE WEAK.
SHE TRIED. IT DIDN'T WORK.

WEAVE MY HAIR INTO A LOOM AND I WILL BE WEAK.
THAT DIDN'T WORK EITHER!

IF YOU LOVED ME, YOU'D TELL ME THE TRUTH.
IF YOU CUT MY HAIR, I WILL BE WEAK.

AHA!
HER PERSISTENCE OVERCAME HIS RESISTANCE.

A CLOSE SHAVE
NOW VULNERABLE, HIS ENEMIES POUNCED.
GET HIM!
BLINDED BY THE PHILISTINES, DREADLOCKS WAS IMPRISONED, AND BECAME A LAUGHING STOCK.
SHOW US YOUR MUSCLES, STRONG MAN!
BUT DREADLOCKS' HAIR BEGAN TO GROW AGAIN...
IN THE TEMPLE OF THE PHILISTINES' GOD
SERVANT BOY, PLACE MY HAND ON THE PILLAR.
LORD, AVENGE ME FOR MY EYES. LET ME DIE WITH THESE PHILISTINES!
DREADLOCKS FELT HIS STRENGTH RETURNING.
WITH HIS HANDS ON BOTH PILLARS, HE PUSHED WITH ALL HIS MIGHT, AND THE TEMPLE COLLAPSED.
MORE WERE KILLED AT HIS DEATH THAN DURING HIS LIFETIME.

THE OUTSIDER
BETHLEHEM, IN JUDAH
SHE WAS A STRANGER IN A STRANGE LAND.
WHO'S THAT GIRL?
THAT'S RUTH. SHE CAME WITH NAOMI.
AFTER THE DEATH OF HER HUSBAND AND TWO SONS IN MOAB, NAOMI WAS LEFT WITH NOTHING.
DAUGHTERS, IT IS TIME FOR ME TO RETURN HOME TO ISRAEL.
I CAN'T LEAVE YOU.
STAY WITH YOUR PEOPLE. HERE YOU COULD MARRY AGAIN.
NO! YOUR PEOPLE WILL BE MY PEOPLE, AND YOUR GOD WILL BE MY GOD.
ONE DAUGHTER-IN-LAW, ORPAH, STAYED...
...THE OTHER, FIERCE FRIEND, LEFT WITH NAOMI.
TIMES IN ISRAEL WERE TOUGH.
FOR THE POOR, SCAVENGING WAS THE ONLY OPTION.
BUT FIERCE HAD CAUGHT THE EYE OF THE LANDOWNER, BOAZ.
ONLY GATHER FROM MY FIELDS.
THANK YOU.
STAY CLOSE AND MY MEN WILL PROTECT YOU.
WHO AM I THAT YOU SHOULD FAVOR ME?
MAKE SURE FIERCE IS LOOKED AFTER.
YES, MASTER, I WILL SEE TO IT.

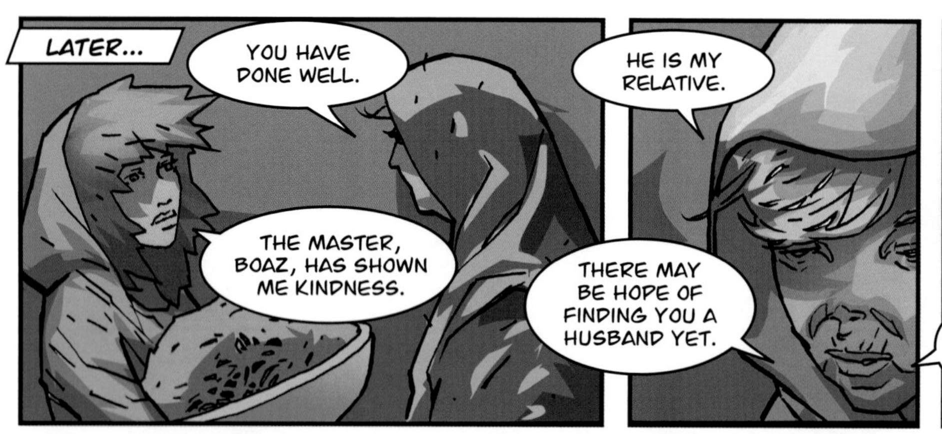
LATER...
YOU HAVE DONE WELL.
THE MASTER, BOAZ, HAS SHOWN ME KINDNESS.
HE IS MY RELATIVE.
THERE MAY BE HOPE OF FINDING YOU A HUSBAND YET.

VISIT HIM TONIGHT. WASH, AND PUT ON YOUR BEST DRESS.

THAT NIGHT
FIERCE QUIETLY MADE HER WAY TO THE PLACE WHERE BOAZ SLEPT.

WHO IS THAT?
IT IS I, FIERCE.
WHAT DO YOU WANT?
MASTER, AS NAOMI'S RELATIVE, WILL YOU BE MY PROTECTOR?

BOAZ WANTED TO FULFIL HIS ROLE AS THE RELATIVE-REDEEMER FOR NAOMI AND MARRY FIERCE.
BUT ANOTHER RELATIVE WAS IN THE WAY.
BOAZ, WHAT ARE YOUR INTENTIONS TOWARD NAOMI AND THIS YOUNG LADY?
I WANT TO BE REDEEMER FOR NAOMI AND MARRY FIERCE, BUT MY RELATIVE HERE MUST DECIDE WHAT HE WANTS.
I CANNOT DO IT. FIERCE IS YOURS.

AND SO BOAZ BECAME THE RELATIVE-REDEEMER AND MARRIED FIERCE.

FIERCE AND BOAZ HAD A SON, OBED, WHOSE GRANDSON DAVID WOULD ONE DAY BECOME THE KING OF ISRAEL.

LISTEN

ELKANAH HAD TWO WIVES. HANNAH HAD NO CHILDREN BUT PENINNAH HAD GIVEN HIM MANY SONS AND DAUGHTERS.

PENINNAH TORMENTED HANNAH.
AREN'T YOU A PITIFUL WIFE!

HA HA HA!

YOU ARE GREATLY LOVED. DON'T WORRY THAT WE HAVE NO CHILD.

AT THE TEMPLE
SOB SOB
LORD, WHY HAVE YOU CURSED ME TO BE BARREN? IF YOU GIVE ME A SON, I WILL GIVE HIM TO YOU.
WHAT?! A WOMAN DRUNK IN THE TEMPLE?

I AM NOT DRUNK. I AM SAD.
GOD HAS HEARD YOUR PRAYER.

AND SOON HANNAH WAS BLESSED, AND WAS WITH CHILD.

WHAT SHALL WE CALL HIM?
SAMUEL, BECAUSE IT MEANS "GOD HAS HEARD".

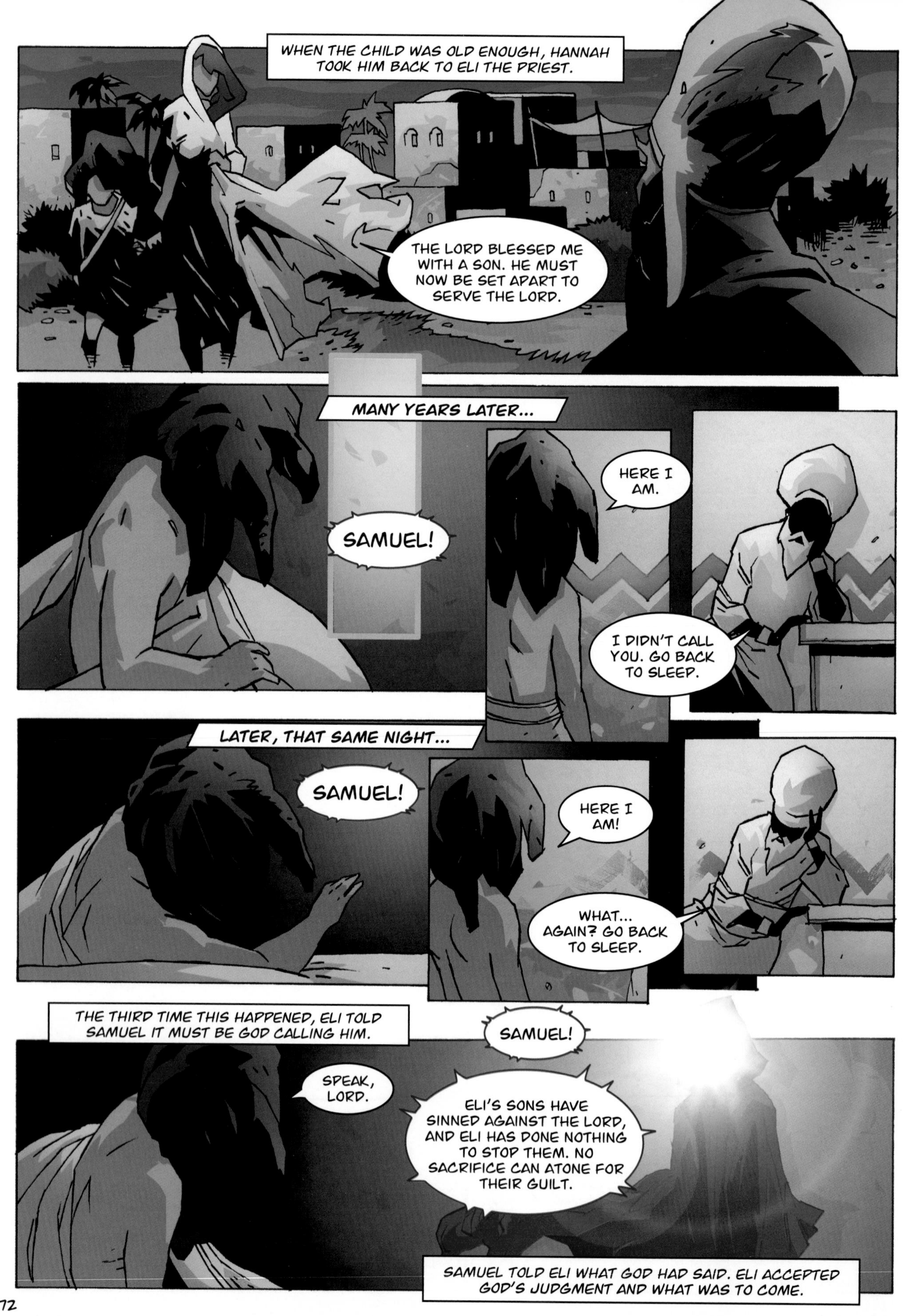
WHEN THE CHILD WAS OLD ENOUGH, HANNAH TOOK HIM BACK TO ELI THE PRIEST.
THE LORD BLESSED ME WITH A SON. HE MUST NOW BE SET APART TO SERVE THE LORD.
MANY YEARS LATER...
SAMUEL!
HERE I AM.
I DIDN'T CALL YOU. GO BACK TO SLEEP.
LATER, THAT SAME NIGHT...
SAMUEL!
HERE I AM!
WHAT... AGAIN? GO BACK TO SLEEP.
THE THIRD TIME THIS HAPPENED, ELI TOLD SAMUEL IT MUST BE GOD CALLING HIM.
SAMUEL!
SPEAK, LORD.
ELI'S SONS HAVE SINNED AGAINST THE LORD, AND ELI HAS DONE NOTHING TO STOP THEM. NO SACRIFICE CAN ATONE FOR THEIR GUILT.
SAMUEL TOLD ELI WHAT GOD HAD SAID. ELI ACCEPTED GOD'S JUDGMENT AND WHAT WAS TO COME.

THE MAN WHO WOULD BE KING
LATER...
SAMUEL ASSEMBLED ALL THE PEOPLE OF ISRAEL AT MIZPAH AND PRAYED FOR THEM.
IF YOU WANT TO RETURN TO THE LORD, YOU MUST RID YOURSELVES OF FOREIGN GODS, AND COMMIT YOURSELVES TO HIM. THEN HE WILL DELIVER YOU FROM THE PHILISTINES.
WE HAVE SINNED AGAINST THE LORD.
WHILE SAMUEL MADE SACRIFICES, THE PHILISTINES ATTACKED. BUT THEY WERE REPELLED BY THE ISRAELITES.
AS SAMUEL GREW OLDER, THE PEOPLE BEGAN TO LOOK FOR A NEW LEADER.
WE WANT A KING LIKE THE OTHER NATIONS!
HAVE YOU REJECTED THE LORD AS KING?
A HUMAN KING WILL BE A SELFISH RULER, AND ONLY ENRICH A FEW AT THE COST OF MANY. YOU WILL CRY OUT TO BE DELIVERED FROM SUCH TYRANNY.
BUT THE PEOPLE HAD SET THEIR HEARTS ON A KING.

SON OF THE SOUTH
SAUL OF THE TRIBE OF BENJAMIN STOOD TALL AMONG HIS PEERS. A WHOLE HEAD TALLER IN FACT. TALL TOWER.
WHERE ARE MY FATHER'S DONKEYS WHICH WERE TIED UP THERE?
A PROPHET LIVES IN THE TOWN NEARBY. LET'S ASK HIM.
ON THEIR WAY TO THE TOWN, THEY MET SAMUEL.
THE LORD HAD REVEALED TO SAMUEL THAT HE WOULD BE VISITED THAT DAY BY THE MAN WHO WOULD BE KING.
WHERE IS THE PROPHET?
I AM THE PROPHET.
GO ON AHEAD OF ME TO THE HIGH PLACE. YOU SHALL EAT WITH ME TODAY.
THE NEXT DAY SAMUEL, THE ANOINTER, POURED OIL OVER TALL TOWER'S HEAD.
THE PEOPLE HAVE ASKED FOR A KING. THE LORD HAS ANOINTED YOU TO LEAD ISRAEL INTO THEIR INHERITANCE.
LONG LIVE THE KING!

NEWLY CROWNED, TALL TOWER LED HIS ARMY TO RESCUE THE PEOPLE OF JABESH-GILEAD WHO WERE BEING BESIEGED BY INVADING AMMONITES.

DIVIDING HIS FORCES INTO THREE, HE ATTACKED THE ENEMY CAMP AT DAWN. AND THE SLAUGHTER CONTINUED UNTIL MIDDAY.

THE PHILISTINES CONTINUED TO HARASS THE LAND.
TALL TOWER HAD A SON, JONATHAN, A DARING FIGHTER.
ISRAEL'S MORALE WAS LOW. JONATHAN WAS READY TO FIGHT, BUT THE REST OF THE ARMY HAD SENT THEIR SWORDS AND SPEARS AWAY FOR SHARPENING.
I'LL TEACH THOSE RAIDERS THAT THERE IS NO PLACE IN THIS LAND FOR THEM.
JUST LET ME AT THEM!
JONATHAN WAS DREAMING OF ACTION. BUT NO ONE ELSE WAS... APART FROM HIS ARMOR BEARER.

WE MUST
CRUSH THEM.
YOU MUST DO WHAT
YOUR HEART TELLS
YOU. I AM WITH YOU.

PERHAPS THE LORD
WILL ACT FOR US. GOD
CAN WIN WITH MANY
MEN OR JUST A FEW.

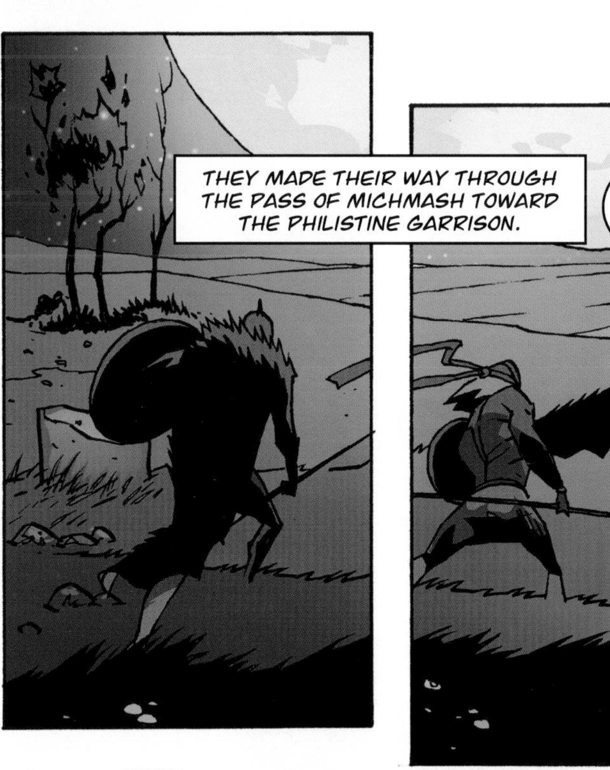
THEY MADE THEIR WAY THROUGH
THE PASS OF MICHMASH TOWARD
THE PHILISTINE GARRISON.
IF THEY SHOW ANY
SIGN THAT THEY DO
NOT FEAR US, WE
WILL TAKE THEM.

WHO GOES
THERE?
JUST US TWO
ISRAELITES.
COME ON UP,
IF YOU THINK YOU
ARE HARD ENOUGH!

CHARGE!
I'LL COVER YOU.
ONE BY ONE, THE PHILISTINES IN THE GARRISON FELL BEFORE JONATHAN.
THEY WERE ALL POWERLESS AGAINST HIM.
AARGH!

IN THE ISRAELITE CAMP
LISTEN! THERE IS FIGHTING IN THE ENEMY GARRISON.
THE ALARM WAS SOUNDED.
THE ONCE-CONFIDENT ENEMY STARTED TO PANIC.

IN THE CONFUSION, THE PHILISTINES STARTED TO ATTACK EACH OTHER.
REALIZING THEIR OPPORTUNITY, THE ISRAELITE ARMY RESPONDED.
COME ON! LET'S FINISH THEM OFF.
THOUGH OUTNUMBERED AND WITH FEW WEAPONS, THE ISRAELITES GAINED THEIR VICTORY. JONATHAN'S DARING HAD BEEN REWARDED.

KING NO LONGER
MANY BATTLES LATER...
THE ANOINTER CAME TO TALL TOWER.
LISTEN, TALL TOWER. I WAS SENT BY THE LORD TO ANOINT YOU AS KING. NOW HEAR WHAT THE LORD COMMANDS.
YOU MUST GO AND DESTROY THE AMALEKITES AND ALL THAT BELONGS TO THEM.
TALL TOWER DEFEATED THE ENEMY, BUT HE KEPT THE BEST OF THEIR POSSESSIONS AND TOOK THEIR KING PRISONER.
WHY HAVE YOU SPARED THEIR KING AND LIVESTOCK?
I THOUGHT IT WOULD PLEASE THE PEOPLE AND THE LORD.
YOU DID NOT COMPLETE THE MISSION. OBEDIENCE IS BETTER THAN ANY SACRIFICE.
YOU REJECTED GOD'S WORD, AND NOW HE REJECTS YOU AS KING.
I HAVE SINNED. MAY GOD FORGIVE ME. COME BACK WITH ME.
NO, I WILL NOT. AND JUST AS YOU HAVE TORN THIS ROBE, SO YOUR KINGDOM WILL BE TORN FROM YOU.
THE KINGDOM OF ISRAEL WILL GO TO A BETTER MAN THAN YOU. YOU ARE FINISHED.

THE SHEPHERD BOY

BATTLECAMP
ISRAEL'S OLD ENEMY, THE PHILISTINES, WERE ON THE RAMPAGE. SHEPHERD BOY'S BROTHERS WERE CALLED AWAY TO JOIN THE FIGHT. BUT THERE WAS A NEW THREAT ON THE BATTLEFIELD.
HEY, I HAVE PROVISIONS FROM OUR FATHER!
GOOD. BUT IT'S DANGEROUS HERE. GO BACK TO OUR SHEEP.
WHO'S THAT MAN?
IT'S GOLIATH THE GIANT. THE KING HAS PROMISED A GREAT REWARD TO THE ONE WHO KILLS HIM.
I WANT TO HELP.
YOU?! NO CHANCE!
BUT WORD OF HIS EAGERNESS SPREAD. EVENTUALLY TALL TOWER SUMMONED SHEPHERD BOY TO HIM.
I WANT TO FIGHT, YOUR MAJESTY.
HA! YOU'RE JUST A LAD.
I CAN FIGHT OFF ANY BEAST, AND, WITH THE LORD'S HELP, I WILL FIGHT THIS PHILISTINE.
THE VALLEY OF DEATH
SO THIS IS YOUR BEST FIGHTER...A BOY WITH A STICK?
I COME TO YOU IN THE NAME OF THE GOD OF ISRAEL. ON THIS DAY I WILL FEED YOUR CORPSE TO THE BIRDS.

ROAR!
WHIRRRR!
THWACK!
AARGH!
THE LORD HAS TRIUMPHED!
TALL TOWER REWARDED SHEPHERD BOY WITH HIGH RANK, AND HE LED HIS MEN TO MANY VICTORIES.
AS SHEPHERD BOY'S RENOWN GREW, TALL TOWER DESCENDED INTO A PIT OF DESPAIR.
GOD WAS ABANDONING HIM.
ONLY SHEPHERD BOY'S MUSIC COULD BRING ANY RELIEF.
THE LORD IS MY SHEPHERD, I SHALL NOT WANT.

LATER...
THE MADNESS OF KING SAUL
THEY SAY THAT I HAVE KILLED THOUSANDS OF MEN, BUT THAT SHEPHERD BOY HAS SLAIN TENS OF THOUSANDS.
HE TRIUMPHS WHEREVER I SEND HIM. AND THE PEOPLE LOVE HIM FOR IT.
BUT TALL TOWER'S SON, JONATHAN, BLOOD BROTHER, REVELED IN SHEPHERD BOY'S VICTORIES.
YOU ARE THE INSPIRATION FOR OUR PEOPLE AND THE HOPE OF THE NATION.
I SOLEMNLY PLEDGE TO YOU: THE BOND OF OUR FRIENDSHIP WILL NEVER BE BROKEN.

THE BOND BETWEEN BLOOD BROTHER AND SHEPHERD BOY RAN DEEP.
MY SON, YOUR FRIENDSHIP WITH SHEPHERD BOY WILL RUIN OUR FAMILY AND YOUR RISE TO THE THRONE.
BEWARE, MY FRIEND. MY FATHER SEES YOU AS A THREAT.
NOW TALL TOWER WAS DETERMINED TO DO EVERYTHING IN HIS POWER TO BE RID OF SHEPHERD BOY.
FATHER, HE HAS DONE NO WRONG TO YOU. HE HAS WON GREAT VICTORIES FOR ISRAEL.
WE MUST PROTECT THE FAMILY.
BUT NOT BY KILLING HIM. ISRAEL NEEDS HIM TO KEEP US UNITED AND OUR ENEMIES AT BAY.
HE SERVES THIS NATION AND YOUR THRONE IN SPITE OF THE RISK TO HIS OWN LIFE.
AND WE ARE LIKE BROTHERS.
AS LONG AS HE IS ALIVE, YOU CANNOT SUCCEED ME AS KING.

ONE DAY TALL TOWER WAS OVERCOME BY JEALOUSY AND DESPAIR.
DIE, YOU UPSTART!
SHEPHERD BOY HAD TO FLEE IN FEAR OF HIS LIFE.
I CANNOT GO BACK. THE KING WILL SURELY KILL ME.
NOB, CITY OF THE LEVITES
ARRIVING AT NOB, SHEPHERD BOY WAS ALONE, HUNGRY, AND UNARMED.
THE PRIESTS ALLOWED HIM TO EAT HOLY BREAD AND THEY GAVE HIM GOLIATH'S SWORD, WHICH THEY HAD KEPT.
SOME TIME LATER, THE ANOINTER DIED. TALL TOWER DEEPLY FEARED THE PHILISTINES.
SO IN DISGUISE HE CONSULTED THE WITCH OF ENDOR.
I SEE A MAN COMING.
IT IS ANOINTER EMERGING FROM HIS GRAVE.
BUT YOU HAVE TRICKED ME. YOU ARE THE KING!
I WILL NOT HARM YOU. WHAT DOES HE SAY?
BECAUSE OF YOUR DISOBEDIENCE, THE LORD HAS TAKEN YOUR KINGDOM FROM YOU AND GIVEN IT TO SHEPHERD BOY.
TOMORROW YOU AND YOUR SONS

SHEPHERD KING
THE NEXT DAY...
OVERWHELMED BY THE PHILISTINES, TALL TOWER KNEW THAT HIS FATE WAS SEALED...

...AND WAS CHASED FROM THE BATTLEFIELD.

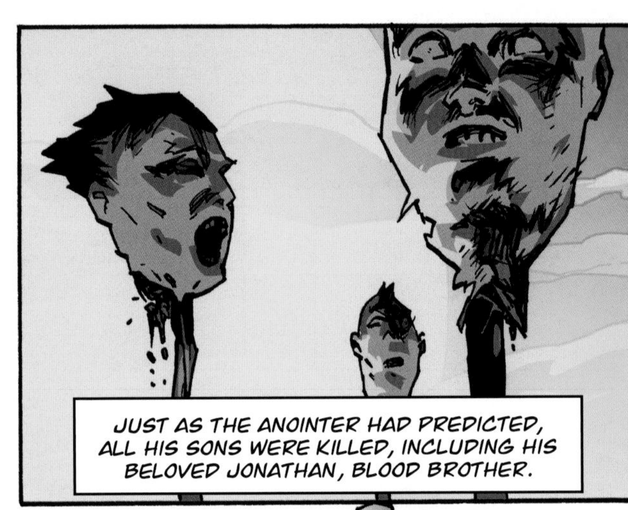
JUST AS THE ANOINTER HAD PREDICTED, ALL HIS SONS WERE KILLED, INCLUDING HIS BELOVED JONATHAN, BLOOD BROTHER.

IT IS OVER.
AARGH!

SHEPHERD BOY WAS CROWNED **SHEPHERD KING**. FIRST OF JUDAH, LATER OF THE WHOLE OF ISRAEL.
AND HE MADE JERUSALEM HIS CAPITAL.
THE ARK OF THE COVENANT WAS CARRIED INTO THE CITY, AND SHEPHERD KING CELEBRATED BEFORE THE LORD.

UNFAITHFUL

SOME WEEKS LATER...

TO COVER HIS SINS, SHEPHERD KING RESOLVED THAT URIAH HAD TO DIE.

HE SENT HIM TO THE FRONT LINE ON AN IMPOSSIBLE MISSION. WITH INEVITABLE RESULTS.

AND THE PROPHET RECALLED ALL OF SHEPHERD KING'S SINS.
"THE BLOOD OF URIAH CRIES OUT AGAINST YOU. YOU CALLED HIM BACK HOME FROM THE FRONT LINE OF A BATTLE THAT YOU SHOULD HAVE BEEN LEADING. IT WAS A TRAP."

"BUT HE WAS MORE NOBLE THAN YOU. HE DID NOT GO HOME TO HIS WIFE..."

"...BUT SLEPT IN THE DOORWAY OF THE PALACE IN THE SERVICE OF HIS KING."

"YOU EVEN GOT HIM DRUNK."

"BUT HE REMAINED AT YOUR SIDE."

"SO YOU INSTRUCTED YOUR MEN TO DO YOUR DIRTY WORK AT THE FRONT LINE."

"BE WARNED, YOUR MAJESTY. GOD KNOWS THAT IT WAS YOUR HAND THAT KILLED URIAH THAT DAY."
I HAVE SINNED AGAINST THE LORD.

"THE LORD WILL SPARE YOUR LIFE, BUT YOUR CHILD WILL DIE. THE SWORD WILL NEVER LEAVE YOUR HOUSE."

TROUBLED TIMES

DAVID'S MIGHTY MEN

THE WISE KING
SHEPHERD KING DIED, AND HIS SON SOLOMON TOOK CHARGE OF THE KINGDOM.
IN A DREAM, HE WAS VISITED BY GOD.
ASK FOR WHATEVER YOU WANT.
I DON'T NEED FAME.
I DON'T NEED MONEY.
BUT I DO NEED WISDOM IN ORDER TO LEAD YOUR PEOPLE.

SOLOMON'S WISDOM BECAME LEGENDARY. WISE MAN.
THAT'S MY BABY.
NO, IT'S MINE!
I TELL YOU, IT'S MINE! IT HAS MY EYES.
NO, YOUR MAJESTY, IT'S MINE. I PROMISE.
SEEING AS YOU ARE BOTH THE MOTHER...
...CUT HIM IN HALF. YOU CAN HAVE HALF EACH.
OH NO, MY LORD! GIVE HIM TO HER. PLEASE SPARE THE BABY'S LIFE.
STOP! GIVE HIM TO HER. SHE IS HIS MOTHER.

THE TEMPLE

WISE MAN STARED OVER JERUSALEM.

NOW THAT WE HAVE PEACE, I MUST DO WHAT MY FATHER WANTED. I MUST BUILD A HOUSE OF WORSHIP TO THE LORD.

AND WISE MAN BECAME THE MASTER BUILDER.

WE WILL BUILD A TEMPLE FOR THE LORD. BRING ME THE BEST STONE FROM OUR QUARRIES AND THE FINEST CEDAR FROM LEBANON.

THE FAME OF WISE MAN'S WISDOM AND RICHES SPREAD.
THE QUEEN OF SHEBA CAME TO SEE FOR HERSELF.
WELCOME TO MY KINGDOM!
I HAVE HEARD SO MUCH ABOUT YOU.
VERY IMPRESSIVE!
BUT WISE MAN HAD A WEAKNESS.
...LED HIM AWAY FROM THE LORD TO FOREIGN GODS AND IDOLS.
AND IN HIS L
DAYS, WISE
ENDED UP A

GAME OF TWO THRONES
WISE MAN DIED.
AND HIS SON REHOBOAM SUCCEEDED HIM AS KING.
BECAUSE OF WISE MAN'S UNFAITHFULNESS AND IDOLATRY, GOD TOLD HIM THAT THE KINGDOM OF ISRAEL WOULD BE TAKEN AWAY FROM HIM AND DIVIDED.
ENVOYS FROM THE NORTHERN TRIBES ARRIVED AT SHECHEM.
UNDER YOUR FATHER WE WERE TAXED HEAVILY. LOWER THE TAX SO THAT OUR PEOPLE CAN SURVIVE.
GIVE ME THREE DAYS AND I WILL GIVE YOU MY RULING.
THREE DAYS LATER, JEROBOAM AND THE ENVOYS RETURNED.
WHAT IS YOUR ANSWER, YOUR MAJESTY?
MY ANSWER IS NO! IN FACT, I WILL RAISE TAXES EVEN HIGHER!
WHAT MORE CAN WE SHARE WITH THE HOUSE OF THE SHEPHERD KING? YOU ARE ON YOUR OWN NOW!
SO THE KINGDOM WAS DIVIDED: JUDAH AGAINST THE REST OF ISRAEL. THE GAME OF THRONES HAD BEGUN.

THE WHOLE COUNTRY WAS TEETERING ON THE BRINK OF CIVIL WAR. JEROBOAM IN THE NORTH VERSUS REHOBOAM IN THE SOUTH.
THROUGH A MESSENGER, GOD TOLD KING REHOBOAM TO HOLD BACK FROM ATTACKING THE NORTHERN TRIBES.
RETREAT!
JEROBOAM WAS CROWNED KING OF THE NORTHERN TRIBES, KING OF ISRAEL.
THE PEOPLE WANT TO WORSHIP GOD.
I WILL BUILD SHRINES IN THE NORTH SO THEY WON'T BE TEMPTED TO RETURN TO THE SOUTH AND TO JERUSALEM.
JEROBOAM MADE TWO GOLDEN CALVES AND PLACED THEM IN DAN AND IN BETHEL.
HERE ARE YOUR GODS WHO BROUGHT YOU OUT OF EGYPT! WORSHIP THEM!

THE KINGS WHO FOLLOWED JEROBOAM IN THE NORTHERN KINGDOM WERE NO BETTER.
WHEN AHAB AND HIS WIFE JEZEBEL ACCEDED TO THE THRONE, THEY TOOK ISRAEL TO NEW LOWS.
THEY BUILT AN ALTAR TO ANOTHER GOD, BAAL.
GOD'S ANGER WAS STIRRED, AND HE SENT HIS PROPHET ELIJAH, RAINMAKER, TO GIVE AHAB A MESSAGE.
BECAUSE OF YOUR WICKEDNESS, AHAB...
...NO RAIN WILL FALL ON THE WHOLE LAND.
ONLY AT MY WORD...
...WILL THE RAINS COME AGAIN.
THERE WERE DRY WELLS AND DRY MOUTHS FROM ONE END OF THE LAND TO THE OTHER.
RAINMAKER HID TO THE EAST OF THE JORDAN RIVER.
RAVENS BROUGHT HIM FOOD AND HE DRANK FROM A STREAM.
AFTER TWO YEARS OF DROUGHT, GOD TOLD HIM TO RETURN TO AHAB.
MAKE UP YOUR MINDS! CAN'T YOU DECIDE WHO TO SERVE?
IF THE LORD IS GOD, FOLLOW HIM. BUT IF BAAL IS GOD, FOLLOW HIM!

ON MOUNT CARMEL
ONE PROPHET AGAINST 450. ONE BULL FOR EACH SIDE.
PREPARE THE BULLS FOR SACRIFICE. THE GOD WHO ANSWERS BY FIRE IS THE TRUE GOD. YOU GO FIRST.
THERE WAS SHOUTING AND DANCING. SEVERAL HOURS WENT BY.
O BAAL, ANSWER US!
WHAT'S WRONG? IS BAAL BUSY?
IS HE TRAVELING? OR SLEEPING? SHOUT LOUDER!
NO RESPONSE. NO REPLY. THE PRIESTS OF BAAL COLLAPSED AND GAVE UP. EXHAUSTED.
NOW SOAK MY ALTAR WITH WATER!
AGAIN!
AND AGAIN!
O LORD GOD OF OUR FATHERS, OF FAITHMAN, LAUGHTER, AND CONTENDER.
REVEAL TODAY THAT YOU ARE GOD IN ISRAEL, AND THAT I AM YOUR SERVANT.
ANSWER ME, O LORD, SO THAT THESE PEOPLE MAY KNOW YOU ARE THE LORD GOD, AND TURN THEIR HEARTS BACK TO YOU.

KABOOM!
A BLAZE OF FIRE CONSUMED RAINMAKER'S OFFERING.
SEIZE THOSE PROPHETS! NO ONE GETS AWAY!
THE GOD OF ISRAEL IS THE LORD OF ALL!
NOW RAINMAKER PRAYED FOR RAIN TO FALL ON THE LAND.
AND HE WAITED...

...AND WAITED.
CLOUDS GATHERED IN THE DISTANCE.
THEN...
CRASH!
RIDE, AHAB, RIDE! BACK TO THAT WIFE OF YOURS!
THE HAND OF THE LORD CAME UPON RAINMAKER.
RUNNING LIKE THE WIND, HE BEAT AHAB BACK TO THE TOWN OF JEZREEL.
AT HIS WORD, THE RAINS HAD COME, AND THE LAND WAS FERTILE AGAIN.
BUT AFTER GETTING DEATH THREATS FROM JEZEBEL, RAINMAKER FLED SOUTH TO JUDAH.

EARTHQUAKE, WIND, AND FIRE

RAINMAKER FOUND PROPHET MAN, ELISHA. HE WAS PLOUGHING WITH THE TWELFTH PAIR OF HIS MANY OXEN.
PROPHET MAN, THE LORD GOD NEEDS YOU!
COME WITH ME.
HUH?
COME!
I WILL. BUT LET ME SAY GOODBYE TO MY PARENTS.
YOU MAY GO, I'M NOT STOPPING YOU. BUT REMEMBER GOD'S CALL.
I WILL.
PROPHET MAN WENT HOME AND SLAUGHTERED ALL HIS OXEN. HE COOKED THE MEAT AND GAVE IT TO HIS NEIGHBORS. THEN HE FOLLOWED RAINMAKER.

CHARIOTS OF FIRE
KING AHAB WAS DEAD. RAINMAKER HAD NOT YET ANOINTED HAZAEL KING OF ARAM OR JEHU KING OF ISRAEL. THIS WOULD BE LEFT TO PROPHET MAN. IT WAS NOW TIME FOR RAINMAKER TO GO.
THEY CAME TO THE JORDAN RIVER.
RAINMAKER TOOK HIS CLOAK AND STRUCK THE WATER. IT PARTED.
RAINMAKER AND PROPHET MAN CROSSED OVER DRY GROUND.
WHAT CAN I DO FOR YOU BEFORE I GO?
GIVE ME A DOUBLE PORTION OF YOUR POWER!
WHOOSH!
WOW!
A CHARIOT OF FIRE IN A WHIRLWIND! AND RAINMAKER WAS GONE.
RAINMAKER!
NOW IT WAS PROPHET MAN'S TURN TO TAKE ON THE MANTLE.

DOUBLE PORTIONS
PROPHET MAN BROUGHT BLESSINGS ON THOSE WHO HONORED THE LORD AND HIS PROPHET.
FIRST TO THE PEOPLE OF JERICHO.
BY THIS BOWL OF SALT, THE LORD WILL RESTORE HEALTH TO THIS SPRING WATER.
MAY THERE BE A GOOD HARVEST!
THEN TO A FOREIGN WOMAN WHO GAVE HIM FOOD AND SHELTER EVERY TIME HE PASSED BY.
TO A GENERAL WITH LEPROSY WHO HUMBLY OBEYED THE PROPHET'S WORDS, HEALING FROM HIS AFFLICTION.
AND TO A NEWLY GRIEVING WIDOW, SALVATION FROM HER CREDITORS.
LOOK, YOUR SON IS NOT DEAD! YOUNG MAN, ARISE!
GO AND WASH IN THE JORDAN!
TAKE THE LITTLE OIL YOU HAVE LEFT AND THE LORD WILL USE IT TO FILL UP AS MANY JARS AS YOU CAN BORROW...
...THEN SELL THE OIL AND PAY YOUR DEBTS!
HA HA HA! GO AWAY, BALDY MAN!
MAY THE LORD CURSE YOU BECAUSE OF YOUR DISHONOR!
RAAAHH!
BUT DOUBLE TROUBLE TO ANYONE SHOWING DISRESPECT TO THE LORD AND HIS PROPHET.

THE CHILDREN OF FAITHMAN WERE NOW A DIVIDED AND REBELLIOUS PEOPLE.
IN SEARCH OF AN OBEDIENT PEOPLE
THE KINGS OF THE SOUTH MOSTLY FOLLOWED IN THE SHEPHERD KING'S WAYS, FAITHFUL TO THE LORD AND HIS COVENANT. BUT THOSE OF ISRAEL IN THE NORTH WERE WHOLLY UNFAITHFUL.
GOD SENT WARNINGS...
THE PROPHET HOSEA MARRIED AN ADULTERESS, YET HE STILL LOVED HER...TO DEMONSTRATE THAT ISRAEL HAD BEEN FAITHLESS BUT WAS STILL LOVED BY GOD.
AMOS THE SHEPHERD RAILED AGAINST ISRAEL'S IDOLATRY, GREED, AND INJUSTICE... BEHAVIOR WHICH WOULD FORFEIT GOD'S PROTECTION.
POOR JONAH, THE RUNNER, WAS SENT TO CALL NINEVAH TO REPENTANCE.
TO THE EAST, THE EMPIRE OF ASSYRIA WAS GROWING IN STRENGTH, GOBBLING UP ANY COUNTRY WHICH STOOD IN ITS WAY.
NO AMOUNT OF PROTECTION MONEY COULD STOP ASSYRIA'S AMBITION.
AND SO THE NORTHERN KINGDOM FELL, AND THE PEOPLE WERE DRAGGED OFF INTO EXILE.

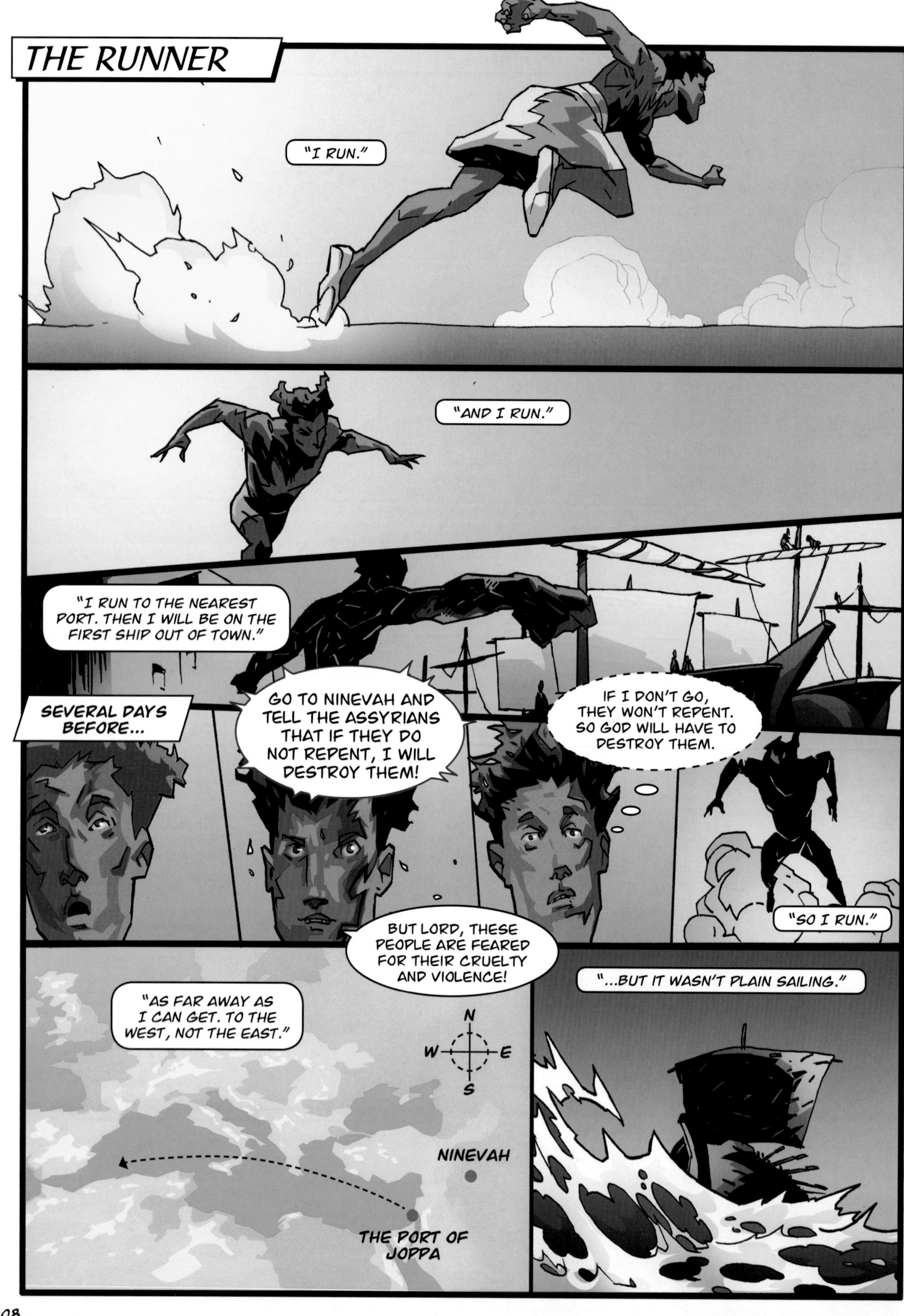
THE RUNNER
"I RUN."
"AND I RUN."
"I RUN TO THE NEAREST PORT. THEN I WILL BE ON THE FIRST SHIP OUT OF TOWN."
SEVERAL DAYS BEFORE...
GO TO NINEVAH AND TELL THE ASSYRIANS THAT IF THEY DO NOT REPENT, I WILL DESTROY THEM!
BUT LORD, THESE PEOPLE ARE FEARED FOR THEIR CRUELTY AND VIOLENCE!
IF I DON'T GO, THEY WON'T REPENT. SO GOD WILL HAVE TO DESTROY THEM.
"SO I RUN."
"AS FAR AWAY AS I CAN GET. TO THE WEST, NOT THE EAST."
N
W
E
S
NINEVAH
THE PORT OF JOPPA
"...BUT IT WASN'T PLAIN SAILING."

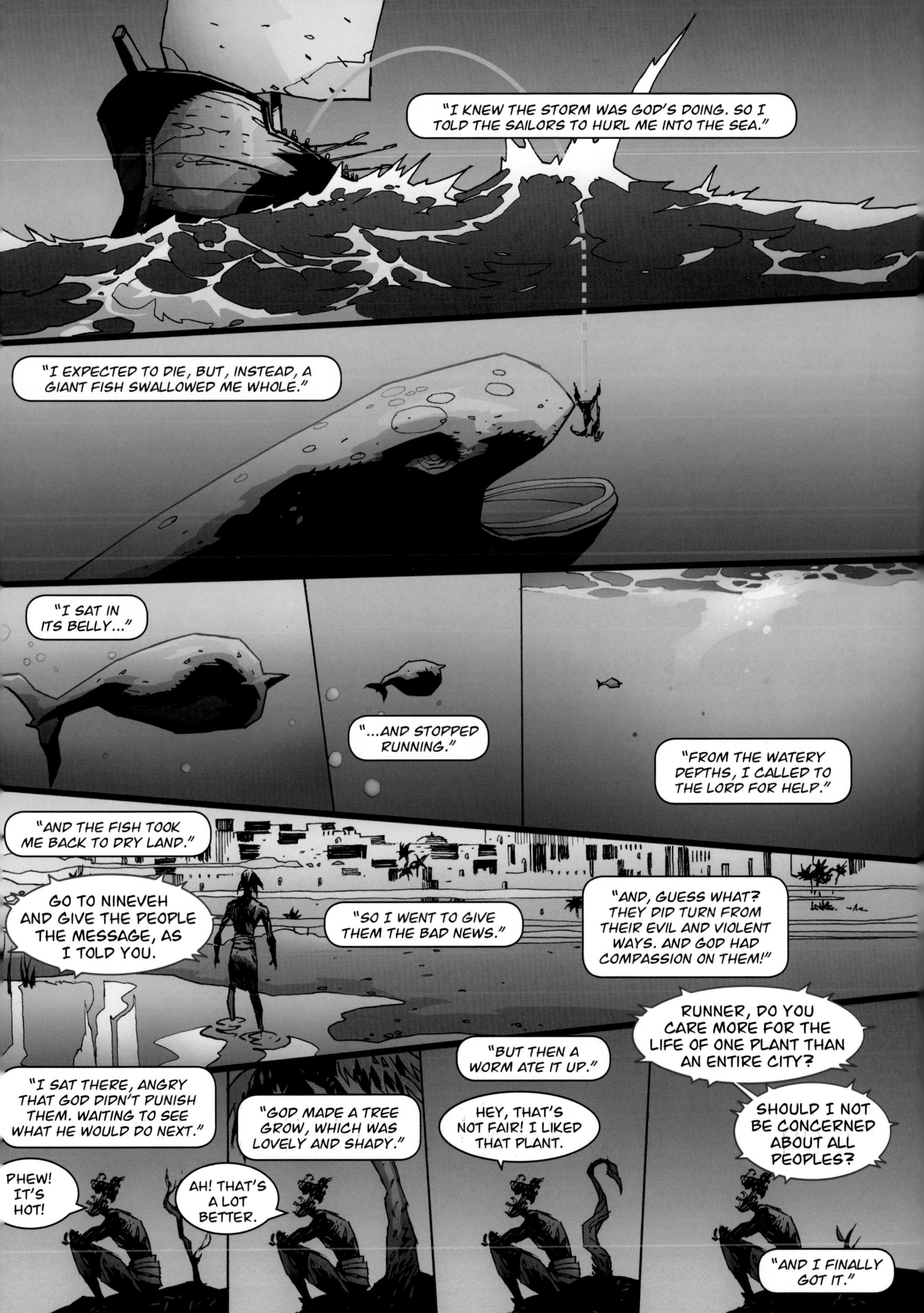
"I KNEW THE STORM WAS GOD'S DOING. SO I TOLD THE SAILORS TO HURL ME INTO THE SEA."
"I EXPECTED TO DIE, BUT, INSTEAD, A GIANT FISH SWALLOWED ME WHOLE."
"I SAT IN ITS BELLY..."
"...AND STOPPED RUNNING."
"FROM THE WATERY DEPTHS, I CALLED TO THE LORD FOR HELP."
"AND THE FISH TOOK ME BACK TO DRY LAND."
GO TO NINEVEH AND GIVE THE PEOPLE THE MESSAGE, AS I TOLD YOU.
"SO I WENT TO GIVE THEM THE BAD NEWS."
"AND, GUESS WHAT? THEY DID TURN FROM THEIR EVIL AND VIOLENT WAYS. AND GOD HAD COMPASSION ON THEM!"
"I SAT THERE, ANGRY THAT GOD DIDN'T PUNISH THEM. WAITING TO SEE WHAT HE WOULD DO NEXT."
PHEW! IT'S HOT!
"GOD MADE A TREE GROW, WHICH WAS LOVELY AND SHADY."
AH! THAT'S A LOT BETTER.
"BUT THEN A WORM ATE IT UP."
HEY, THAT'S NOT FAIR! I LIKED THAT PLANT.
RUNNER, DO YOU CARE MORE FOR THE LIFE OF ONE PLANT THAN AN ENTIRE CITY?
SHOULD I NOT BE CONCERNED ABOUT ALL PEOPLES?
"AND I FINALLY GOT IT."

THE VISIONARY
WHEN THE NORTH FELL, THE SOUTHERN KINGDOM OF JUDAH CONTINUED TO HOLD OUT AGAINST THE ASSYRIANS. BUT FOR HOW LONG?
IN THE YEAR KING UZZIAH DIED, ISAIAH, THE VISIONARY, WAS WORSHIPING IN THE TEMPLE, WHEN HE HAD A VISION.
HOLY, HOLY, HOLY IS THE LORD OF HOSTS; THE WHOLE EARTH IS FULL OF HIS GLORY!
WOE IS ME! I AM A MAN OF UNCLEAN LIPS AND I LIVE AMONG UNCLEAN PEOPLE. YET I HAVE SEEN THE LORD!
LOOK, THIS COAL HAS TOUCHED YOUR LIPS; YOUR GUILT HAS GONE NOW, AND YOUR SIN IS BLOTTED OUT.
WHO WILL SPEAK FOR US?
HERE I AM! SEND ME!
THIS IS WHAT THE VISIONARY SAID:
INHABITANTS OF JERUSALEM AND PEOPLE OF JUDAH! THE LORD HAS TENDED YOU LIKE A BEAUTIFUL VINEYARD, BUT YOU HAVE PRODUCED ONLY BAD FRUIT.
YOU HAVE PURSUED WEALTH AND HAVE BUILT GREAT HOUSES. YOU PARTY HARD, BUT DON'T HONOR GOD'S WAYS. YOU CALL EVIL GOOD, AND GOOD EVIL. GOD LOOKS FOR JUSTICE, BUT HE SEES ONLY BLOODSHED AND CRIES OF DISTRESS.
ASSYRIA IS AT HAND. BUT IT IS THE LORD YOU SHOULD FEAR!

DEATH AT THE DOOR
KING HEZEKIAH OF JUDAH WAS A GOOD KING, FAITHFUL TO THE LORD.
LORD, YOU SEE THIS GREAT ARMY AT THE GATES. THEY HAVE CONQUERED NATIONS WHOSE GODS ARE JUST WOOD AND STONE.
NOW I PRAY THAT YOU WILL DELIVER US FROM THEM, SO THAT ALL MAY KNOW THAT YOU ARE THE ONE TRUE LORD GOD.
ENTER THE VISIONARY
YOUR MAJESTY, THE LORD HAS HEARD YOUR PRAYER.
GOD WILL SHOW THESE ASSYRIANS WHO IS REALLY IN CHARGE.
IT IS GOOD. THE LORD HAS HEARD OUR PRAYER AND RECOGNIZED OUR FAITHFULNESS.
THAT NIGHT THE ANGEL OF THE LORD DESCENDED UPON THE CAMP OF THE ASSYRIANS AND SLAUGHTERED 185,000 MEN. THE KING FLED BACK TO ASSYRIA.
THOUGH THE FALL OF JUDAH WAS AVERTED, THE VISIONARY STILL WARNED ITS INHABITANTS TO TURN AWAY FROM THEIR WICKEDNESS AND STAY LOYAL TO THEIR GOD.
ASSYRIA WAS NO LONGER THE THREAT. NOW IT WAS BABYLON.

THE REFORMATION KING

THE CRYING MAN
JERUSALEM. JEREMIAH, CRYING MAN. IN A VAULTED DUNGEON...
"BEFORE I WAS FORMED IN THE WOMB, YOU KNEW ME. YOU SET ME APART TO BE A PROPHET TO THE NATIONS AND MY CITY. YOU GAVE ME THE WORDS TO SPEAK AND ACTIONS TO PERFORM."
"I HAVE TOLD THEM YOUR WORDS OF JUDGMENT AND OF HOPE, AND YET THEY HATE ME."
"I STOOD AGAINST THE PRIESTS AND PROPHETS WHO LIED IN YOUR NAME, AND WHO CLAIMED THAT JERUSALEM WOULD NEVER FALL TO BABYLON."
"THEY WERE MY BROTHERS BUT NOW THEY ARE MY ENEMIES."
"TRUSTING IN YOU HAS MADE ME PUBLIC ENEMY NUMBER ONE. I HAVE SET BEFORE THEM THE CHOICE OF LIFE AND DEATH: LIFE, IF THEY SURRENDER AND CHANGE THEIR WAYS, BUT SURELY DEATH IF THEY CHOOSE TO RESIST THE INVADER."

PREVIOUSLY...AT THE PALACE, DURING THE REIGN OF KING ZEDEKIAH, SON OF KING JOSIAH
TELL ME, CRYING MAN, IS THERE ANY WORD FROM THE LORD? WILL HE PERFORM MIRACLES FOR US, AS IN THE PAST?
NO, YOUR MAJESTY. THE LORD IS ABOUT TO TURN AGAINST YOU.
WITH HIS OUTSTRETCHED ARMS, THE LORD MADE THE EARTH, ALL NATIONS, AND ALL LIVING THINGS.
BUT JUST AS I A WEARING THIS YOKE, SO YOU UNDER THE BABYL YOU AND EVERY AROUND YOU
IN OUTRAGE AND DEFIANCE THE FALSE PROPHETS BROKE THE YOKE.
YOU MAY BREAK A YOKE OF WOOD BUT THE GOD OF ISRAEL WILL PUT AN IRON YOKE UPON YOU.
THE LORD WILL THIS NATION LIKE A JAR IS SMAS BEYOND RE
YOU CAN PUT STOCKS AND TELL TH MAD, BUT IT WILL WORDS FROM CO

AS FOR YOU, YOUR MAJESTY, YOU WILL LIVE. BUT ONLY SO YOU CAN SEE THE FURY OF THE LORD POURED OUT ON THIS CITY AS A RESULT OF YOUR REBELLION, AND ITS PEOPLE TAKEN OFF TO BABYLON IN EXILE.
"WHENEVER I SPOKE, IT WAS OF JUDGMENT AND DESTRUCTION. WORDS FROM THE LORD, BUT ONES WHICH BROUGHT ME INSULT AND DERISION. AND NOW I AM CAST INTO THE SLUDGE AT THE BOTTOM OF A CISTERN TO DIE."
"THEN...RELIEF AS A SERVANT OF THE KING ARRIVED TO RESCUE ME."
"FREED, I COULD NOW DECLARE A MESSAGE OF HOPE AMID THE GLOOM: IN 70 YEARS TIME THE CAPTIVES WOULD RETURN FROM EXILE IN BABYLON."
YOUR MAJESTY, ONE DAY A RIGHTEOUS BRANCH WILL SPROUT FROM THE SHEPHERD KING'S FAMILY TREE.
THE LORD WILL MAKE A NEW COVENANT WITH HIS PEOPLE, AND HIS LAW WILL BE WRITTEN ON THEIR HEARTS. HE WILL BE THEIR GOD AND THEY HIS PEOPLE.
BUT NOT BEFORE THE CITY FALLS, AND THE TEMPLE IS DESTROYED. BABYLON WILL BE TRIUMPHANT.

INTO EXILE
THE SONS OF JOSIAH WERE NOTHING LIKE THEIR FATHER. BACK TO THE OLD WAYS OF POLITICAL INTRIGUE AND REFUSAL TO ACCEPT THE WARNINGS OF GOD'S PROPHETS.
THE JUDGMENT OF JUDAH'S HISTORIANS: THE SONS DID EVIL IN THE SIGHT OF GOD.
NO TRUE REPENTANCE. NO JUSTICE FOR THE POOR. NO RESPECT FOR THEIR COVENANT WITH THE GOD OF ISRAEL. IN THEIR PLACE, OPPRESSION, IDOLATRY, AND FAITHLESSNESS.
KING NEBUCHADNEZZAR WAS ALL-CONQUERING. NATION AFTER NATION FELL BEFORE THE BABYLONIAN ARMIES ON THEIR WAY TO EGYPT. JERUSALEM WAS JUST ONE SMALL OBSTACLE IN THEIR PATH.

SO EVENTUALLY JERUSALEM FELL TOO, AND GOD'S JUDGMENT CAME UPON THE CITY. THE PEOPLE SUFFERED FOR THE STUBBORNNESS OF KING ZEDEKIAH WHO HAD REFUSED TO LISTEN TO CRYING MAN AND FOLLOW THE WAY OF PEACE BY SUBMITTING HIMSELF TO GOD.
KING ZEDEKIAH FLED, BUT HE DID NOT GET FAR.
AS A HORRIFYING REMINDER OF HIS SHORT-SIGHTEDNESS, THE BABYLONIANS EXECUTED HIS SONS, THEN BLINDED HIM, AND LED HIM STUMBLING AS A CAPTIVE TO BABYLON.
THE CITY AND THE TEMPLE BURNED. ITS RICHES WERE CARTED AWAY. A NEW WAVE OF JUDEANS WERE LED OFF AS PRISONERS INTO HUMILIATING EXILE.

THE WATCHMAN
MEANWHILE, ALREADY EXILED IN BABYLON, THE PRIEST EZEKIEL, WATCHMAN, WAITED.
"I SAW A VISION OF GOD."
SUDDENLY CAME WIND, LIGHTNING, AND FIRE.
IN THE FIRE, FOUR LIVING BEINGS LIKE MEN, BUT EACH WITH FOUR WINGS AND FOUR FACES: A LION, AN OX, AN EAGLE, AND A MAN.
AND, HARD TO DESCRIBE, WHEELS TURNING UPON WHEELS.
THEIR WINGS MADE A SOUND LIKE ROARING WATER, LIKE THE VOICE OF ALMIGHTY GOD.
WATCHMAN! TAKE THIS SCROLL AND EAT IT. THEN GO AND SPEAK TO THE CHILDREN OF ISRAEL.

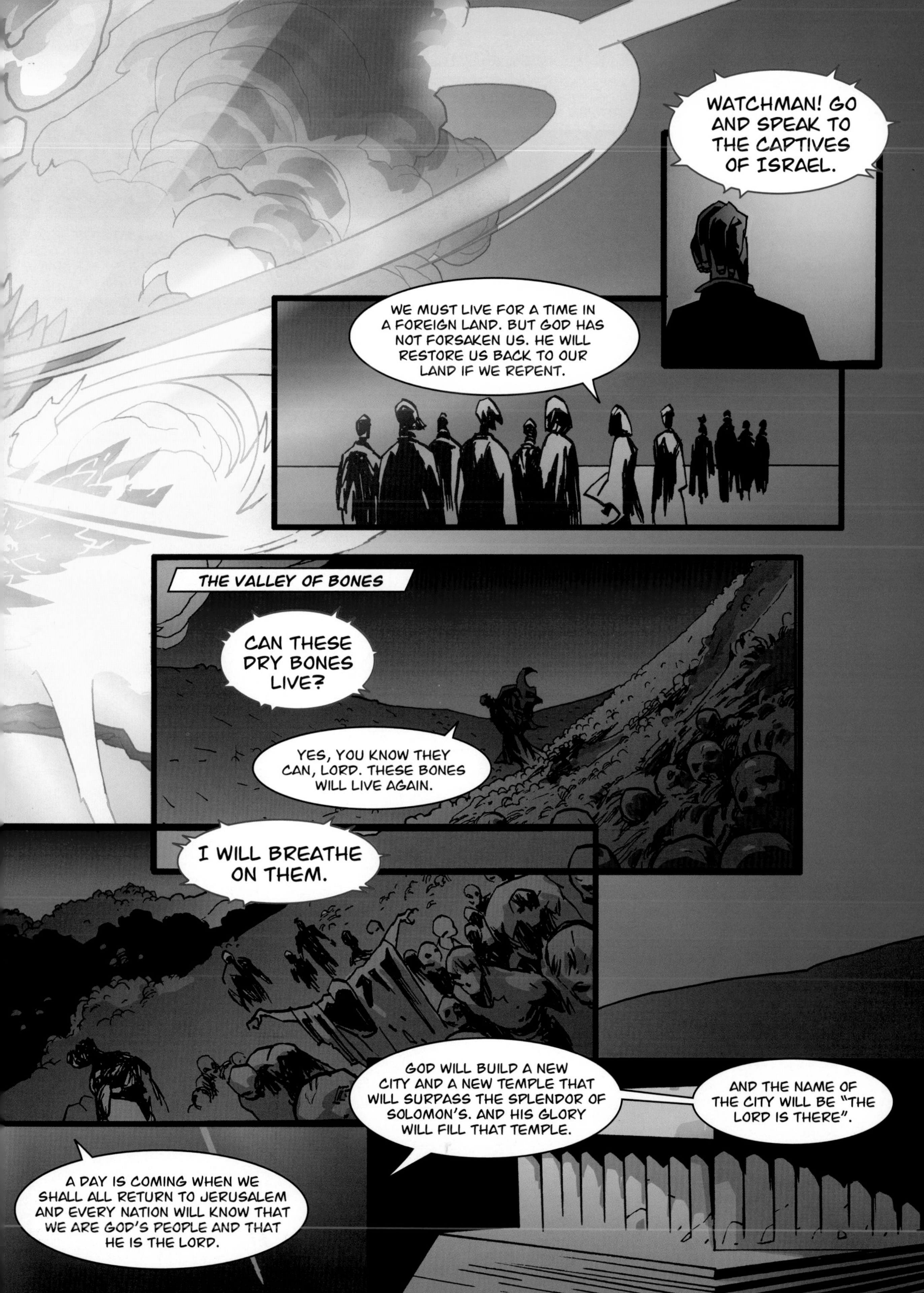
WATCHMAN! GO AND SPEAK TO THE CAPTIVES OF ISRAEL.
WE MUST LIVE FOR A TIME IN A FOREIGN LAND. BUT GOD HAS NOT FORSAKEN US. HE WILL RESTORE US BACK TO OUR LAND IF WE REPENT.
THE VALLEY OF BONES
CAN THESE DRY BONES LIVE?
YES, YOU KNOW THEY CAN, LORD. THESE BONES WILL LIVE AGAIN.
I WILL BREATHE ON THEM.
GOD WILL BUILD A NEW CITY AND A NEW TEMPLE THAT WILL SURPASS THE SPLENDOR OF SOLOMON'S. AND HIS GLORY WILL FILL THAT TEMPLE.
AND THE NAME OF THE CITY WILL BE "THE LORD IS THERE".
A DAY IS COMING WHEN WE SHALL ALL RETURN TO JERUSALEM AND EVERY NATION WILL KNOW THAT WE ARE GOD'S PEOPLE AND THAT HE IS THE LORD.

EXILED
AS KING NEBUCHADNEZZAR'S STRANGLEHOLD ON JERUSALEM TIGHTENED, HUNDREDS OF CAPTIVES WERE TAKEN BACK TO BABYLON.
SOME OF THE BRIGHTEST AND THE BEST FROM THE FIRST WAVE OF HOSTAGES WERE SELECTED TO SERVE IN THE BABYLONIAN PALACE. THESE INCLUDED A YOUNG MAN NAMED DANIEL AND HIS THREE FRIENDS.
OVER THE NEXT DECADE VAST NUMBERS OF THEIR COMPATRIOTS WERE ALSO TAKEN INTO EXILE.
NEBUCHADNEZZAR HAD NOW EXTENDED THE BABYLONIAN EMPIRE EVEN FURTHER.
HE WAS A MASTER OF THE UNIVERSE.
BUT HE WAS UNNERVED BY A DREAM...
...WHICH DEEPLY TROUBLED HIM.
THE DREAM WAS OF A GIANT STATUE MADE OF DIFFERENT METALS: GOLD AT THE TOP, THEN SILVER, BRONZE, AND IRON. AND AT THE BOTTOM, FEET MADE OF IRON AND CLAY.
A MASSIVE ROCK FELL FROM THE SKY AND STRUCK THE FEET OF THE STATUE, DESTROYING IT. THE ROCK THEN BECAME A HUGE MOUNTAIN.
I DREAMED SOMETHING TERRIFYING LAST NIGHT. YOU MUST TELL ME WHAT IT WAS AND ITS MEANING.
THE WISE MEN AND MAGICIANS WERE STUMPED.
YOUR MAJESTY, ONLY THE GODS THEMSELVES COULD DO SUCH A THING.
YOU SHALL TELL ME THE DREAM AND ITS MEANING UPON PAIN OF DEATH. YOU HAVE ONE DAY.

TOTAL RECALL

THE FOLLOWING DAY

YOUR MAJESTY, THE LORD HAS REVEALED THAT YOU SAW A GREAT STATUE.

THE HEAD WAS MADE OF GOLD, AND THIS IS YOUR KINGDOM. GOD OF HEAVEN HAS MADE YOU RULER.

AFTER YOUR KINGDOM WILL COME THREE MORE KINGDOMS...SILVER, BRONZE, AND IRON. THE FEET OF IRON AND CLAY FORETELL A KINGDOM WITH BOTH STRENGTHS AND WEAKNESSES.

BUT THE GOD OF HEAVEN WILL ESTABLISH ANOTHER KINGDOM, AND THIS IS THE MEANING OF THE ROCK THAT TURNED INTO A MOUNTAIN. THIS REIGN WILL LAST FOREVER.

YOUR GOD IS THE GOD OF ALL GODS AND THE REVEALER OF MYSTERIES. YOU HAVE SAVED MANY LIVES TODAY. YOU SHALL BE CHIEF OF ALL MY WISE MEN.

FOR MANY YEARS DANIEL SERVED BABYLON FAITHFULLY. BUT, AS HE PREDICTED, NEBUCHADNEZZAR'S DYNASTY ENDED, WITH THE MEDES AND THE PERSIANS TAKING OVER HIS EMPIRE. DANIEL NOW SERVED A NEW MASTER.

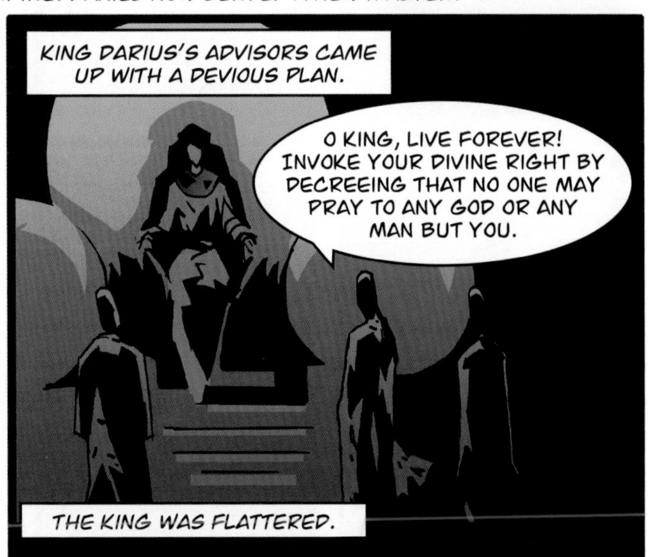

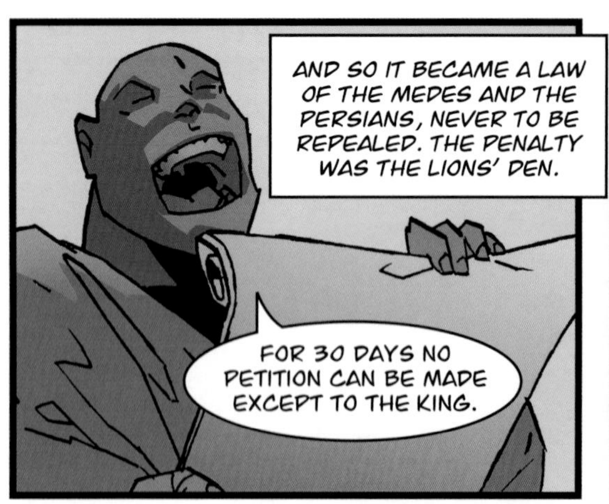
AND SO IT BECAME A LAW OF THE MEDES AND THE PERSIANS, NEVER TO BE REPEALED. THE PENALTY WAS THE LIONS' DEN.
FOR 30 DAYS NO PETITION CAN BE MADE EXCEPT TO THE KING.

LORD GOD OF ISRAEL! I HONOR YOU ALONE AS MY CREATOR, AS LORD OF THE WHOLE EARTH. I PRAY THAT THIS NATION WILL TURN TO YOU.

WE FOUND DANIEL, **RESISTER**, PRAYING TO HIS GOD. HE MUST BE PUNISHED.

RESISTER IS NOT AN ENEMY OF THIS NATION...
...BUT THE LAW IS BINDING.

AT THE LIONS' DEN
MAY HIS GOD HAVE MERCY ON HIM.

INTO THE DARKNESS...
AARGH!

GOD OF ISRAEL, YOU ARE NOT JUST THE GOD OF LIGHT.

YOU ARE THE GOD THAT RULES OVER DARKNESS.

AND I, YOUR SERVANT, WILL NOT BE CUT OFF FROM YOUR GOODNESS.

HEAR THIS! THE ENTIRE WORLD SHALL KNOW THAT THE GOD OF RESISTER IS THE TRUE GOD WHOSE REIGN WILL NEVER END.

RESISTER HAD A VISION OF HIS OWN WHERE GOD SHOWED HIM THE FATE OF ALL THE EMPIRES TO COME.

THE ANCIENT OF DAYS TOOK HIS PLACE ON THE THRONE, WHITE AS SNOW, FLAMING WITH FIRE. THE COURT WAS SET. THE BOOKS WERE OPENED.

THEN I SAW ONE LIKE A SON OF MAN, COMING WITH THE CLOUDS OF HEAVEN, AND APPROACHING THE ANCIENT OF DAYS. HE WAS GIVEN AUTHORITY, GLORY, AND POWER AND HIS REIGN WILL BE EVERLASTING.

THE KINGDOM OF GOD THE MOST HIGH WILL BE EVERLASTING, AND ALL RULERS WILL WORSHIP AND OBEY HIM.

STAR WOMAN

DURING THE EXPANSION OF THE PERSIAN EMPIRE, JEWS WERE DISPERSED THROUGHOUT THE LAND.
INCLUDING TO THE CITY OF SUSA...WHERE KING AHASUERUS WAS THROWING A BANQUET. WHICH QUEEN VASHTI REFUSED TO ATTEND.
WHAT DO YOU MEAN, SHE WON'T COME?!

FIND ME A NEW QUEEN!

UH...?

THE BIGGEST BEAUTY PAGEANT IN THE LAND BEGAN.
ALL THE WOMEN WHO HAVE BEEN SELECTED MUST REPORT TO THE PALACE.

A JEWISH MAN NAMED MORDECAI VISITED HIS ADOPTED DAUGHTER, ESTHER. SHE WAS A STAR BEAUTY.
DEAREST **STAR**, YOU HAVE BEEN CHOSEN.

IF YOU BECOME QUEEN, MAYBE GOD WILL SHOW GREAT KINDNESS TO OUR PEOPLE.
BUT SAY NOTHING OF YOUR HERITAGE FOR NOW.

AT THE PALACE, WOMAN AFTER WOMAN WAS PRESENTED TO THE KING, BUT NOT A SINGLE ONE TOOK HIS FANCY.

BUT THEN...IN CAME STAR.
SHE WILL BE MY QUEEN.

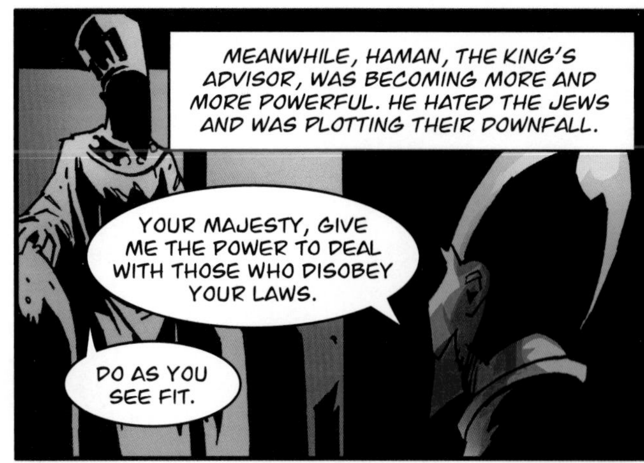
MEANWHILE, HAMAN, THE KING'S ADVISOR, WAS BECOMING MORE AND MORE POWERFUL. HE HATED THE JEWS AND WAS PLOTTING THEIR DOWNFALL.
YOUR MAJESTY, GIVE ME THE POWER TO DEAL WITH THOSE WHO DISOBEY YOUR LAWS.
DO AS YOU SEE FIT.

HAMAN ISSUED A DECREE THAT ON THE THIRTEENTH DAY OF THE TWELFTH MONTH, ALL JEWS WERE TO BE PUT TO DEATH AND THEIR GOODS CONFISCATED.
YOU MUST HELP OUR PEOPLE, FOR WE ARE ALL IN FEAR OF OUR LIVES. PLEAD WITH THE KING!

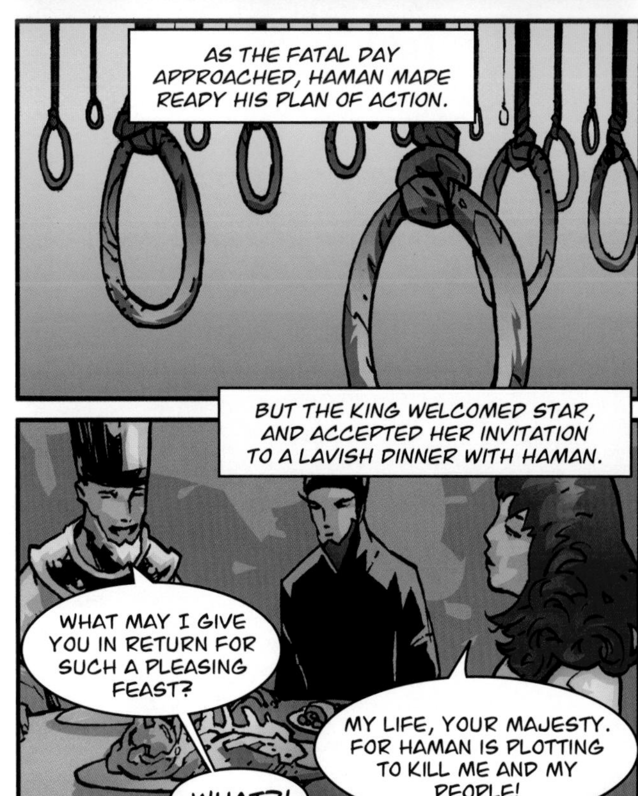
AS THE FATAL DAY APPROACHED, HAMAN MADE READY HIS PLAN OF ACTION.
BUT THE KING WELCOMED STAR, AND ACCEPTED HER INVITATION TO A LAVISH DINNER WITH HAMAN.
WHAT MAY I GIVE YOU IN RETURN FOR SUCH A PLEASING FEAST?
MY LIFE, YOUR MAJESTY. FOR HAMAN IS PLOTTING TO KILL ME AND MY PEOPLE!
WHAT?!

THE CUSTOM AT THAT TIME WAS THAT NO ONE COULD APPROACH THE KING WITHOUT HIS SUMMONS.
IT WAS A CAPITAL OFFENCE. STAR WOULD BE TAKING A HUGE RISK.
MORDECAI, GATHER THE JEWS TO FAST AND PRAY FOR ME.
THEN I WILL GO TO THE KING. IF I PERISH, I PERISH.

THE KING WAS FURIOUS AND HANGED HAMAN ON HIS OWN GALLOWS.

NOW UNDER ROYAL PROTECTION, THE JEWISH PEOPLE WERE SPARED FROM DESTRUCTION.

THE GUARDIANS
AS FORETOLD BY THE PROPHETS, EXILE DID NOT LAST FOREVER. GOD DIRECTED CYRUS, KING OF PERSIA, TO BUILD A TEMPLE IN JERUSALEM.
A DECREE FROM HIS MAJESTY! ALL THOSE WHO WISH TO RETURN TO JERUSALEM TO REBUILD THE HOUSE OF THE LORD MAY DO SO WITH THE BLESSING OF THE KING.
ZERUBABBEL, GRANDSON OF KING ZEDEKIAH, RETURNED TO JERUSALEM ALONG WITH MANY OF HIS COMPATRIOTS. IT WAS THE FIRST TIME THAT JEWS HAD SET FOOT IN THE CITY FOR 70 YEARS. THEY REBUILT THE ALTAR AND LAID THE FOUNDATIONS OF THE TEMPLE. AND SO BEGAN THE LONG TASK OF RECONSTRUCTION.
AFTER MANY YEARS, THE TEMPLE WAS FINALLY FINISHED AND REDEDICATED TO GOD.
WE MUST RESTORE THE WORSHIP OF OUR LORD AND PROMISE OBEDIENCE TO HIS LAW.
BUT WE WILL NOT BE SAFE UNTIL THE WALLS HAVE BEEN REBUILT.
THE JEWS HAD MANY ENEMIES, SUCH AS SANBALLAT THE SAMARIAN, WHO DID NOT WANT TO SEE THEM RESETTLED BACK IN THE LAND.
DO THESE FEEBLE JEWS REALLY THINK THAT THEY CAN REBUILD THEIR CITY?
THESE ADVERSARIES HAMPERED PROGRESS FOR SEVERAL WEEKS, WHILE THE JEWS ARMED THEMSELVES IN ORDER TO BE PREPARED FOR AN ATTACK.

THE GOVERNOR
NEHEMIAH HAD BEEN SERVING ARTAXERXES, THE KING OF PERSIA, BUT RETURNED TO JERUSALEM TO OVERSEE THE REBUILDING OF THE WALLS OF THE CITY.
HALF THE MEN HE PUT TO THE REBUILDING WORK, AND HALF TO DEFENDING THEIR CO-WORKERS AGAINST MARAUDING ATTACKERS.
ARRANGED IN FAMILY GROUPS, EACH FOUGHT TO PROTECT THEIR LOVED ONES AND THEIR HOMES.
IN NO TIME, THE WALLS WERE REBUILT AND THE CITY MADE SAFE.
THE PEOPLE GATHERED, BUT WHEN EZRA THE PRIEST READ OUT FROM THE BOOK OF THE LAW, THEY BEGAN TO WEEP.
THIS IS THE LAW OF THE LORD! DO NOT CRY, FOR THIS DAY IS HOLY TO THE LORD.
THEN NEHEMIAH, NOW **THE GOVERNOR** OF THE CITY, SPOKE TOO.
GO AND EAT, AND SHARE YOUR FOOD WITH THOSE WHO DO NOT HAVE ANY, BECAUSE TODAY IS A FESTIVAL TO THE LORD. AND DO NOT BE SAD. THE JOY OF THE LORD IS OUR STRENGTH.
AMEN! AMEN!

OVER THE YEARS, MORE AND MORE JEWS RETURNED FROM THEIR PLACES OF EXILE TO THE LAND OF JUDAH TO RESETTLE.

THE GOVERNOR HAD LIVED TO SEE THE DAY WHEN THE WALLS OF JERUSALEM WERE REBUILT.

THE SENTINELS

A NEW DAY OF THE LORD
THE RETURN TO JERUSALEM STILL LEFT MANY HOPES UNFULFILLED, AND ISRAEL'S OBEDIENCE FALTERED AGAIN.
AND THEN I WILL COME, AND ALL THE HOLY ONES WITH ME, AND I WILL REIGN OVER THE WHOLE EARTH.
BUT THE STORY DIDN'T FINISH THERE. A NEW GENERATION OF PROPHETS TOLD OF A VISION OF NEW HOPE... WHEN GOD WOULD COME TO BE WITH HIS PEOPLE.
ONE OF THESE PROPHETS WAS A MAN NAMED MALACHI.
LOOK, I AM SENDING MY MESSENGER, AND HE WILL PREPARE A PATH FOR ME. THEN THE LORD, WHO YOU HAVE BEEN LOOKING FOR, WILL SUDDENLY APPEAR!

IRON- OOT EMPIRE
400 YEARS.
400 YEARS SINCE GOD SPOKE.
400 YEARS OF NATIONS RISING.
400 YEARS OF WARS. OF REBELLIONS.
OF OPPRESSION.
400 YEARS OF WAITING, WONDERING, DOUBTING.
WOULD GOD EVER SPEAK AGAIN?

CARNATION

IN THE BEGINNING WAS THE WORD.

AND THE WORD WAS WITH GOD, AND THE WORD WAS GOD.

HE WAS IN THE BEGINNING WITH GOD.

ALL THINGS CAME INTO BEING THROUGH HIM.

AND WITHOUT HIM NOT ONE THING CAME INTO BEING.

AND THE DARKNESS DOES NOT OVERCOME IT.

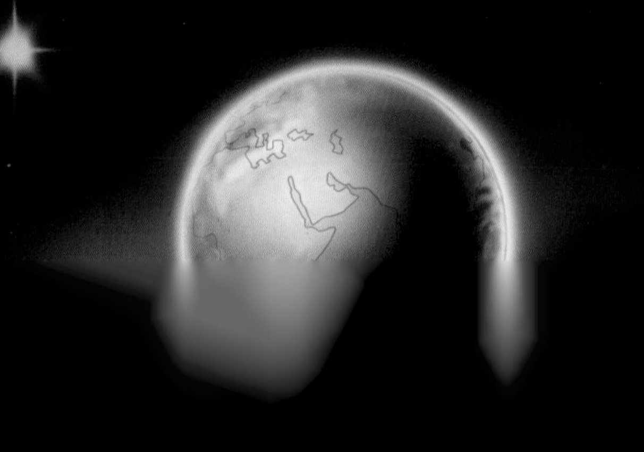

WONDERFUL WOMAN

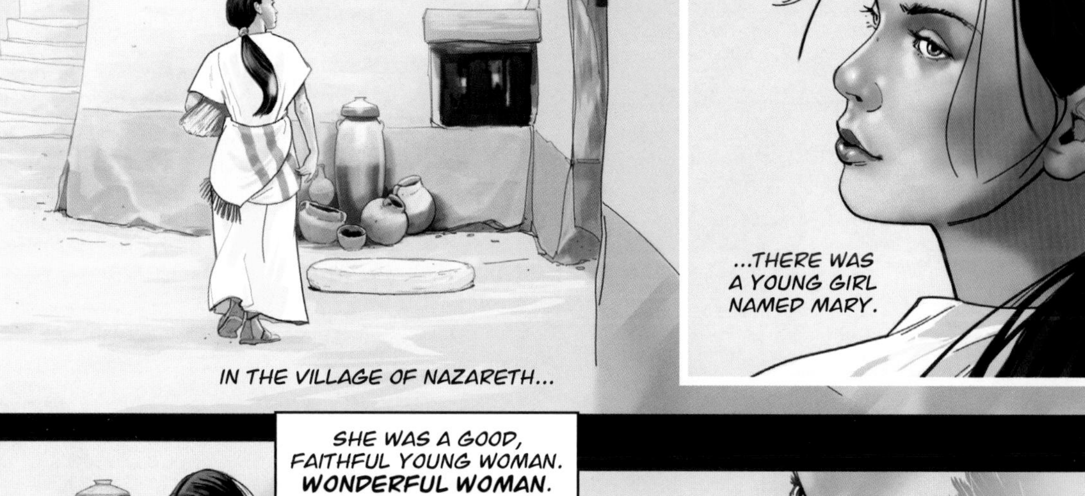

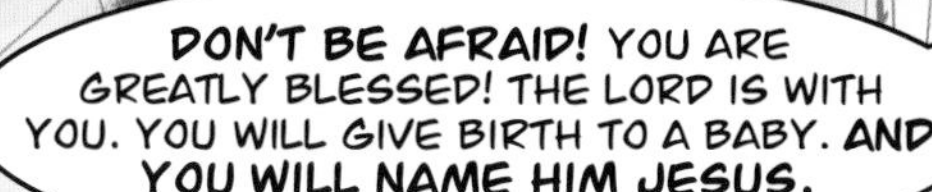

THE HOLY SPIRIT WILL COME DOWN ON YOU. AND GOD'S POWER WILL COME OVER YOU.

FAMILY MAN

JOSEPH, THE DESCENDANT, WAS OF THE LINE OF THE SHEPHERD KING.
HE HAD LONG GIVEN UP ANY HOPE OF MARRIAGE.

SO HIS ENGAGEMENT TO WONDERFUL WOMAN HAD MADE HIS HEART SING.
NOW THE NEWS OF THE BABY BROKE IT.

THE THOUGHT OF PUBLICLY SHAMING HER BROKE IT EVEN MORE.
HE DECIDED TO END THEIR CONTRACT PRIVATELY, WITHOUT ANY SHAME TO WONDERFUL WOMAN.

DESCENDANT!
HE WAS A GOOD MAN. AND THE DESCENDANT WAS ABOUT TO FIND OUT THAT HE, TOO, HAD A PART IN GOD'S PLAN.

DESCENDANT, SON OF THE SHEPHERD KING, DON'T BE AFRAID TO TAKE WONDERFUL WOMAN AS YOUR WIFE. THE CHILD SHE CARRIES WAS CONCEIVED BY THE HOLY SPIRIT.
SHE WILL GIVE BIRTH TO A SON, AND YOU WILL CALL HIM JESUS BECAUSE HE WILL SAVE HIS PEOPLE FROM THEIR SINS.
THE DESCENDANT KNEW THAT ALL THE ANGEL SAID WAS TRUE.
THIS HAPPENED TO FULFIL WHAT THE PROPHET HAD SAID...THAT A VIRGIN WOULD BEAR A SON AND NAME HIM IMMANUEL, "GOD WITH US".

SO WONDERFUL WOMAN AND THE DESCENDANT WERE MARRIED.

DAVID'S CITY

BEFORE WONDERFUL WOMAN GAVE BIRTH, THE EMPEROR AUGUSTUS ORDERED A CENSUS TO BE TAKEN THROUGHOUT THE ROMAN EMPIRE.
EVERYONE WENT TO REGISTER, EACH PERSON TO THEIR OWN TOWN.

THE DESCENDANT AND WONDERFUL WOMAN TRAVELED MANY MILES TO THE PLACE WHERE THEY WERE TO REGISTER...
...BETHLEHEM.
THE TOWN WAS FULL OF NOISE, OF PEOPLE, OF ANIMALS, ALL TRYING TO FIND A PLACE TO REST.
BUT THAT WASN'T EASY.

A ROOM?
I'M SORRY. WE'RE FULL.

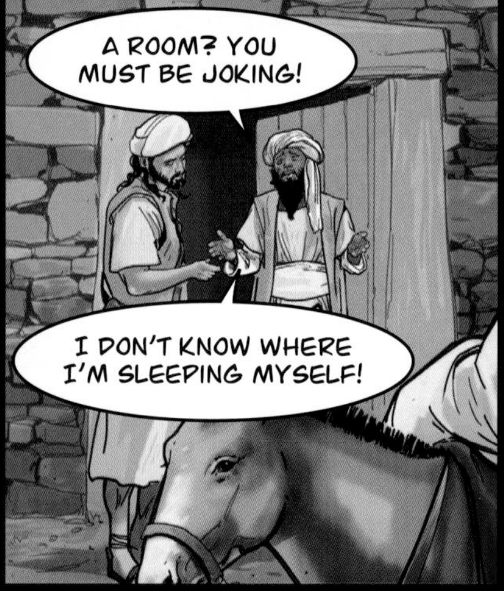
A ROOM? YOU MUST BE JOKING!
I DON'T KNOW WHERE I'M SLEEPING MYSELF!

I'M REALLY SORRY. I HAVE NOTHING. THOUGH...
THERE IS...
WE'LL TAKE ANYTHING.

...THE STABLE.
OH...
I KNOW...BUT IT'S WARM AND DRY, AND YOU PROBABLY WON'T GET ANYTHING ELSE TONIGHT!
WE'LL TAKE IT.

WE'LL GET USED TO THE SMELL.
I DON'T THINK THAT'S GOING TO BE OUR MAIN PROBLEM.

SHEEP-MEN
THAT NIGHT THE BABY WAS BORN.
I'VE GOT MY PIPE. HOW ABOUT A SONG?
IN THE HILLS OUTSIDE BETHLEHEM, SHEPHERDS WERE WATCHING AND GUARDING THEIR SHEEP.
THANKS, JACOB--
AN ANGEL OF THE LORD APPEARED TO THEM.
DO NOT BE AFRAID! I BRING YOU GOOD NEWS. TODAY IN THE TOWN OF THE SHEPHERD KING...
...A SAVIOR HAS BEEN BORN.
AARGH!
WHAT'S THAT!?
HE IS CHRIST THE LORD! THIS WILL BE A SIGN TO YOU: YOU WILL FIND THE BABY WRAPPED IN CLOTHS AND LYING IN A MANGER.
ANGELS. I CAN SEE ANGELS!
GLORY TO GOD IN THE HIGHEST, AND PEACE ON EARTH TO ALL WHO PLEASE HIM!
QUICKLY, QUICKLY.
WE HAVE TO FIND THIS MANGER! AND THE BABY...
HOW DID YOU KNOW TO COME HERE?
THE ANGELS TOLD US.
SO THIS IS OUR SAVIOR, THE MESSIAH, CHRIST THE LORD!

STAR-MEN

MANY MILES AWAY IN THE EAST, WISE MEN TOOK NOTE OF THE SIGNS.
THEY REVEALED THAT A NEW KING OF THE JEWS HAD BEEN BORN.

THEY LOOKED TO THE SKY AND FOLLOWED A STAR.

THEY CAME TO HEROD #1'S PALACE IN JERUSALEM.
GREETINGS, YOUR MAJESTY. WE HAVE COME FAR ON A JOURNEY TO FIND THE KING OF THE JEWS.

I AM THE KING. WHY DO YOU SEEK ME?
YOU? WE ARE SORRY, YOUR MAJESTY. THE ONE WE SEEK IS A BABE!
WE FOLLOW A STAR THAT LEADS TO THE MESSIAH. THE CHOSEN ONE.

REALLY? WELL, SEARCH WELL. AND WHEN YOU FIND HIM, TELL ME.
I WOULD LIKE TO WORSHIP HIM ALSO.
THEY LEFT. NOT TRUSTING THE KING. VOWING NEVER TO TELL HIM ANYTHING.

DO NOT BE AFRAID. WE COME LOOKING FOR THE KING OF THE JEWS.
WE COME TO WORSHIP HIM. AND WE BRING GIFTS.

GOLD, FRANKINCENSE, MYRRH.
GIFTS THE LIKE OF WHICH WONDERFUL WOMAN AND THE DESCENDANT HAD NEVER SEEN BEFORE.
THEY ALSO BROUGHT A WARNING... BEWARE OF HEROD #1.
SO THE FAMILY FLED TO EGYPT.
THEY STAYED THERE UNTIL HEROD #1 DIED.

THE VOICE

THIRTY YEARS LATER
THE RIVER JORDAN
JOHN THE BAPTIST.
TURN AWAY FROM YOUR SINS AND BE BAPTIZED.
JOHN, THE VOICE, WAS THE ONE THE PROPHETS HAD TALKED ABOUT.
AND THIS WAS HIS MESSAGE...
YOU WILL SAY, "WE ARE ABRAHAM'S CHILDREN". THAT MEANS NOTHING. THE AXE IS READY TO CUT DOWN THE TREES. EVERY TREE THAT DOES NOT PRODUCE GOOD FRUIT WILL BE CUT DOWN.
PREPARE A WAY FOR THE LORD!
YOU ARE ALL SNAKES! CHANGE YOUR HEARTS! DISASTER APPROACHES.
BE BAPTIZED IN THE RIVER BY ME.
THERE IS STILL TIME. GOD WILL FORGIVE YOUR SINS.
I'M A TAX COLLECTOR; PEOPLE HATE ME FOR WORKING WITH THE ROMANS. HOW CAN I BE FORGIVEN? WHAT SHOULD I DO?
DON'T TAKE MORE TAXES FROM PEOPLE THAN YOU HAVE BEEN ORDERED TO COLLECT.
ARE YOU THE MESSIAH?
I BAPTIZE WITH WATER. BUT SOMEONE MORE POWERFUL IS COMING. AND I AM NOT GOOD ENOUGH EVEN TO UNTIE HIS SANDALS.
HE WILL BAPTIZE YOU WITH THE HOLY SPIRIT AND FIRE.
FROM VILLAGE TO VILLAGE, NEWS OF THE VOICE SPREAD. AND MANY CAME TO BE BAPTIZED.

AND JESUS, TOO, CAME TO BE BAPTIZED.

THE HEAVENS OPENED... AND A VOICE CALLED OUT.
THIS IS MY SON, WHOM I LOVE. WITH HIM I AM WELL PLEASED!
AFTER HE WAS BAPTIZED, JESUS, **THE SON**, WAS LED BY THE HOLY SPIRIT...
...INTO THE DESERT.

TEMPTATION

THERE HE STAYED FOR FORTY DAYS AND FORTY NIGHTS.

WITHOUT FOOD... WAITING...
JESUS.

...FOR THE ACCUSER.
JESUS, ARE YOU HUNGRY? OF COURSE YOU ARE!

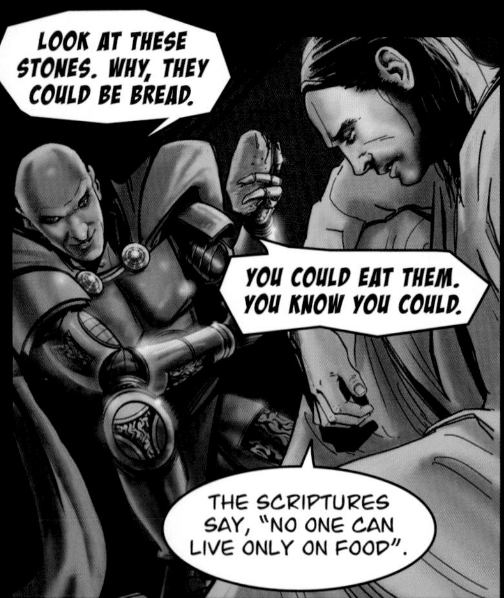
LOOK AT THESE STONES. WHY, THEY COULD BE BREAD.
YOU COULD EAT THEM. YOU KNOW YOU COULD.
THE SCRIPTURES SAY, "NO ONE CAN LIVE ONLY ON FOOD".

I CAN GIVE POWER AND GLORY TO YOU.
IT WAS GIVEN TO ME. I CAN SHARE IT WITH WHOEVER I CHOOSE!

LOOK!
YOU CAN HAVE IT ALL! ALL THE KINGDOMS ON EARTH. JUST BOW DOWN TO ME.
THE SCRIPTURES SAY, "WORSHIP THE LORD YOUR GOD..."

"...AND SERVE ONLY HIM."
THROW YOURSELF FROM THE HIGHEST ROOF OF THE TEMPLE.
GOD WILL NOT LET YOU FALL...
...HE WILL SEND HIS ANGELS TO CATCH YOU IN THEIR ARMS.
YOU WILL NOT FEEL THE STONES ON YOUR FEET!
THE SCRIPTURES SAY, "DO NOT TEST THE LORD YOUR GOD".
GO AWAY, ACCUSER! I WILL NEVER SERVE YOU.
NEVER.
I WILL NOT BE THAT KIND OF KING.
THE ACCUSER HAD FINISHED HIS TESTS. AND HE LEFT THE SON ALONE...FOR NOW.

UNTIL...

COME WITH ME.

I WILL TEACH YOU HOW TO BRING IN **PEOPLE**, INSTEAD OF FISH.

LET'S GO!

THE BROTHERS DROPPED THEIR NETS.

AND WITH JAMES AND JOHN, FISHERMEN AS WELL...

...THEY FOLLOWED THE SON.

THE SON ASKED TWELVE MEN TO FOLLOW HIM, TO BE HIS DISCIPLES.

THE FOUR FISHERMEN: SIMON, WHO THE SON NAMED PETER, ANDREW, JAMES, AND JOHN.

AND MATTHEW, THOMAS, JAMES, SON OF ALPHAEUS, SIMON THE ZEALOT, JUDAS, SON OF JAMES, BARTHOLOMEW, PHILIP, AND JUDAS ISCARIOT.

PEOPLE FROM ALL WALKS OF LIFE.

EVEN A TAX COLLECTOR.

WITH HIS DISCIPLES, THE SON TRAVELED AROUND GALILEE. SPEAKING TO PEOPLE.

PERFORMING MIRACLES. AND TEACHING.

AND AS HE TAUGHT, PEOPLE CAME TO LISTEN.

THE WORD SPREAD, AND PEOPLE CAME...

...IN THEIR HUNDREDS.

IN THEIR THOUSANDS.

WISE MAN

GOD BLESSES THOSE WHO ARE HUNGRY.

THEY WILL BE FED.

THOSE WHO WEEP, GOD WILL BLESS. THEIR TEARS WILL BE TEARS OF JOY.

GOD BLESSES THOSE WHO ARE HATED, REJECTED, AND CALLED EVIL, BECAUSE OF THE SON OF MAN!

HOW TERRIBLE FOR THOSE WHO ARE RICH NOW!

YOU, WHO HAVE HAD AN EASY LIFE.
HOW TERRIBLE FOR YOU WHO ARE FULL NOW.
YOU WILL GO HUNGRY.

HOW TERRIBLE FOR YOU PEOPLE WHO LAUGH NOW.
YOU WILL WEEP...YOU WILL MOURN.
HOW TERRIBLE WHEN PEOPLE SPEAK WELL OF YOU.
THEY DID THE SAME WITH THE FALSE PROPHETS.

LISTEN, I SAY...
LOVE YOUR ENEMIES...DO GOOD TO THOSE WHO HATE YOU. BLESS THOSE WHO CURSE YOU.
PRAY FOR THOSE WHO ILL-TREAT YOU. DO FOR OTHERS JUST AS YOU WOULD HAVE THEM DO FOR YOU.

LOVE YOUR ENEMIES... FORGIVE THEM.

THEN YOUR REWARD WILL BE GREAT!
YOU WILL BE TRUE CHILDREN OF GOD IN HEAVEN.

GOD IS GOOD TO EVERYONE, INCLUDING THE UNGRATEFUL AND THE WICKED.
THE RELIGIOUS LEADERS LEFT. OUTRAGED. THEY HAD NEVER HEARD ANYTHING LIKE IT.

MIDNIGHT CALLER

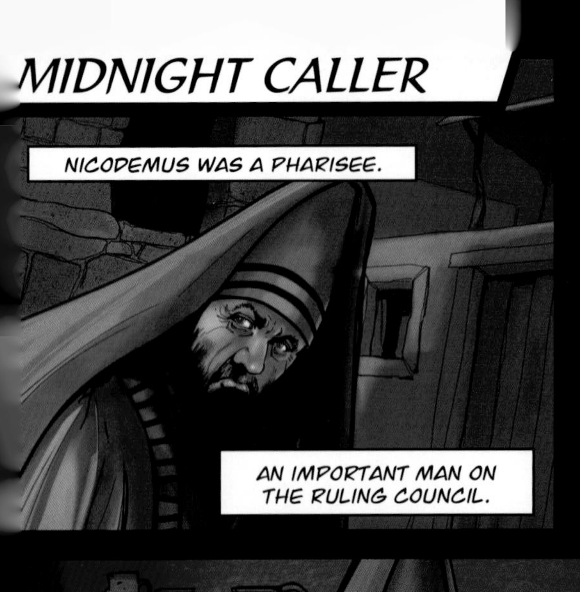

THIRST-SLAYER

THE VOICE'S END

MEANWHILE, JOHN, THE VOICE, WAS A PRISONER OF **HEROD #2**.

HIS CRIME? PUBLICLY DENOUNCING THE KING FOR MARRYING HIS BROTHER'S EX-WIFE, HERODIAS.

HEROD #2 WANTED TO KILL THE VOICE, BUT THE PEOPLE REGARDED HIM AS A PROPHET. THE KING WAS FEARFUL.

UNTIL...

IT WAS THE KING'S BIRTHDAY. THERE WAS A GREAT PARTY.

YOUR HIGHNESS.

IN HONOR OF THIS GREAT DAY, MY DAUGHTER WOULD LIKE TO DANCE FOR YOU.

AND SO SALOME DANCED FOR THE KING.

HEROD #2 WATCHED, HIS EYES HEAVY WITH WINE.

WHICH MAY ACCOUNT FOR WHAT HE SAID NEXT...

I'LL GIVE YOU ANYTHING YOU ASK FOR. I SWEAR, ANYTHING!

GIVE ME, HERE, NOW, THE HEAD OF THE VOICE.

THOUGH FEARFUL, WHAT COULD HE DO...

...BUT SAY YES?

STORM-BREAKER

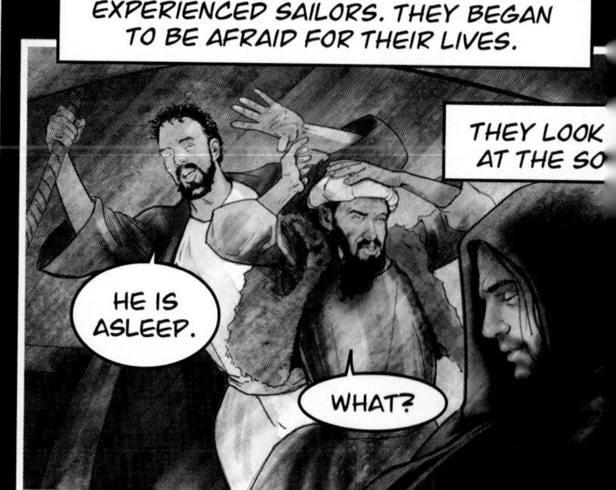

THE EXORCIST

PLEASE, NOT THE ABYSS...
DO NOT SEND US INTO THE ABYSS...
I BEG YOU...
THE PIGS...
INTO THE PIGS...
YES, INTO THEM...
NO ABYSS...
PIGS.
AS YOU WISH.
GO!
THE EVIL SPIRITS LEFT THE MAN.
AND WENT INTO THE PIGS...WHO RUSHED TO THEIR DEATH.
THE PEOPLE OF THE VILLAGE HAD LIVED IN FEAR OF THE MAN LEGION.
BUT WHEN THEY SAW LEGION WELL, THEY BECAME MORE AFRAID...
...OF THE SON, BECAUSE OF WHAT HE HAD DONE.
AND THEY ASKED THE SON TO LEAVE.

MIRACLE MAN
AS HE TRAVELED AND TAUGHT, THE SON HEALED MANY PEOPLE.
THIS CAME TO THE ATTENTION OF A JEWISH OFFICIAL NAMED JAIRUS.
WHOSE DAUGHTER LAY DYING.

TEACHER!

MY DAUGHTER IS ILL, DYING.
PLEASE COME AND LAY YOUR HANDS ON HER, AND I KNOW SHE WILL LIVE.

TAKE ME TO YOUR HOME.

WAIT! SOMEONE TOUCHED ME!
I FELT POWER GO OUT FROM ME.

FORGIVE ME, MASTER.

I THOUGHT IF I COULD JUST TOUCH YOUR CLOAK, I WOULD BE WELL. I HAVE SUFFERED BLEEDING FOR TWELVE YEARS. NO DOCTORS CAN HELP.
HAVE COURAGE, DAUGHTER. YOUR FAITH HAS HEALED YOU.

MAY GOD GIVE YOU PEACE.

JAIRUS' HOUSE
THE MOURNERS' CRIES TOLD EVERYONE THEY WERE TOO LATE.
EXCEPT THE SON.
GET EVERYBODY OUT! SHE IS NOT DEAD, ONLY SLEEPING.
LAUGHTER BROKE OUT AMONG THE CROWD.
DON'T BE FRIGHTENED. HAVE FAITH: YOUR DAUGHTER WILL BE WELL.

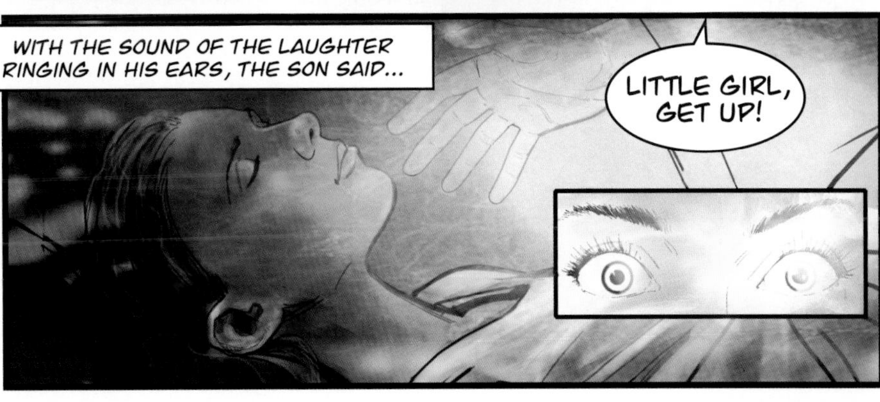
WITH THE SOUND OF THE LAUGHTER RINGING IN HIS EARS, THE SON SAID...
LITTLE GIRL, GET UP!

THIS LITTLE ONE IS HUNGRY.
GIVE HER SOMETHING TO EAT.
THE SON TOLD HER PARENTS NOT TO TELL ANYONE WHAT HAD HAPPENED.

BUT, AS IS THE WAY WITH ALL AMAZING STORIES, THE NEWS SPREAD.
AND MANY MORE PEOPLE CAME LOOKING FOR THE SON TO HEAL THEM.
BLIND PEOPLE, LAME PEOPLE, LEPERS, AND THE POSSESSED. AND WHETHER JEW, GENTILE, MAN, OR WOMAN, ALL WHO CAME WERE HEALED.

THE KING?

AS THE STORIES OF THE SON SPREAD, PEOPLE CAME TO BE HEALED.
BUT ALSO...
...PEOPLE CAME TO HEAR HIM TEACH.
IN THEIR THOUSANDS!
WHICH BROUGHT PROBLEMS...
MASTER...
...THIS IS A REMOTE PLACE, AND IT'S LATE. SEND EVERYONE AWAY TO GET FOOD.
NO NEED TO SEND THEM AWAY. WHY DON'T YOU FEED THEM?
BUT, MASTER, HOW CAN WE FEED ALL THESE PEOPLE?
ALL WE HAVE IS WHAT THIS LAD HAS BROUGHT.
WHICH IS?
FIVE LOAVES AND TWO FISH.
HMM.... SHOULD BE ENOUGH.
AND SO...
...THE SON SAID A PRAYER OF THANKS.
AND THEY SHARED OUT THE FOOD.
EVERYONE ATE THEIR FILL...5,000 PEOPLE! AND THERE WERE TWELVE BASKETS OF FOOD LEFT OVER!
DID YOU SEE THAT? HE MUST BE ONE OF THE PROPHETS. RAINMAKER, MAYBE?
IS HE THE ONE WE'VE BEEN WAITING FOR?
WE COULD CROWN HIM KING! WITH HIS POWER, WHAT CHANCE WOULD THE ROMANS HAVE?
CROWNED KING?
NOT LIKE THIS.

SOME TIME LATER...
THE SON WENT TO BE ALONE TO PRAY.
HIS DISCIPLES WENT BACK TO THEIR BOAT, AND SAILED ACROSS THE LAKE.
GOING DOWN TO THE LAKESIDE, THE SON SAW THEIR BOAT IN THE DISTANCE.
THEY LOOKED IN SOME TROUBLE GOING AGAINST THE WIND.
STEPPING ONTO THE WATER, THE SON DECIDED TO JOIN THEM.
CAUSING A RIPPLE OF FEAR...
LOOK! ON THE WATER! A GHOST!
DON'T BE FRIGHTENED. IT'S ME!
IT'S NOT A GHOST, IT'S THE MASTER!
MASTER, CALL ME. TELL ME TO WALK ON THE WATER.
COME ON, PETER, JOIN ME!
SLOWLY... DON'T LOOK DOWN.
TRY NOT TO THINK ABOUT IT. YOU MIGHT...
...SINK!
HELP!
PETER, DON'T WORRY. I HAVE YOU.
THE WATERS CALMED.
THE DISCIPLES WERE BEGINNING TO UNDERSTAND THE EXTENT OF HIS POWER. COULD HE BE THE SON OF GOD?

A SECRET MESSIAH?

THE TRANSFORMER

A TRUE HERO

NOT EVERYONE WAS CONVINCED BY THE SON. MANY DISTRUSTED HIM. AND WANTED TO TRAP HIM.
TEACHER. WHAT'S THE SECRET TO INHERITING LIFE IN THE AGE TO COME ?
THE SECRET? ARE YOU NOT AN EXPERT?

WHAT DO THE SCRIPTURES SAY?
"LOVE THE LORD YOUR GOD WITH ALL YOUR HEART AND MIND."
AND THAT WE MUST LOVE OUR NEIGHBOR AS WE LOVE OURSELVES.
CORRECT. DO ALL THAT AND YOU WILL RECEIVE THIS NEW LIFE.

BUT, TEACHER...WHO IS OUR NEIGHBOR?
LET ME TELL YOU A STORY.
THERE WAS ONCE A MAN GOING DOWN THE ROAD FROM JERUSALEM TO JERICHO.

...ROBBERS ATTACKED HIM.
AARGH!
AND LEFT HIM FOR DEAD.

ON THE WAY...
A PRIEST COMING ALONG THE ROAD SAW THE MAN. HE THOUGHT HE WAS DEAD...SO HE CROSSED THE ROAD.
AND HURRIED AWAY.

ANOTHER EXPERT IN THE LAW PASSED BY.
HE WOULDN'T TOUCH A DEAD BODY... SO HE RAN OFF QUICKLY.

FINALLY A SAMARITAN CAME BY...A SAMARITAN, HATED BY JEWS.
WHAT DO YOU THINK HE DID?
HE STOPPED, TOOK PITY, BANDAGED THE MAN'S WOUNDS...
... AND PUT HIM ON HIS DONKEY.
AND TOOK HIM TO THE NEAREST INN...
...WHERE HE PAID FOR THE MAN TO BE CARED FOR UNTIL HE WAS WELL.

WHO WAS THE TRUE FRIEND? THE NEIGHBOR?
THE ONE WHO TOOK PITY. WHO SHOWED LOVE.

WELL, GO THEN. AND DO THE SAME.

THE PRODIGAL
HERE IS ANOTHER STORY ABOUT GOD'S LOVE.
THERE WAS ONCE A MAN WHO HAD TWO SONS.
ONE WAS DUTIFUL, HARD-WORKING.
BUT THE YOUNGEST...
THE YOUNGEST SAID...
GIVE ME MY INHERITANCE NOW! I WANT TO GO INTO THE WORLD...SEE IT, HAVE FUN, AND ENJOY MYSELF.
SO HIS FATHER GAVE HIM HIS INHERITANCE, AND OFF HE WENT.
TO "ENJOY HIMSELF". WHICH HE DID.
HE HAD PARTIES, MADE NEW FRIENDS.
MORE PARTIES, GIRLS, AND MORE PARTIES.
HIS NEW FRIENDS LOVED HIM...
...UNTIL THE MONEY RAN OUT.
THEN EVERYONE DISAPPEARED.
HE WAS FORCED TO TAKE WORK LOOKING AFTER PIGS. HE WAS SO HUNGRY HE WAS TEMPTED TO EAT THEIR FOOD.
ONE DAY HE DECIDED TO GO HOME. HE WOULD BEG HIS FATHER TO ACCEPT HIM BACK... AS A SERVANT.
AS HE NEARED THE HOUSE, HIS FATHER RECOGNIZED HIM.
BENEATH THE RAGS AND THE DIRT, HIS FATHER SAW HIS SON.
AND RAN TO HIM.
THE SON SAID...
FATHER, I HAVE SINNED AGAINST YOU AND GOD.
HIS FATHER REPLIED...
YOU'RE HOME! MY SON WHO WAS DEAD IS NOW ALIVE! MY SON WHO WAS LOST IS FOUND!

-GIVER
RUS WAS THE BROTHER
RTHA AND MARY, AND A
RIEND OF THE SON.
MASTER!
LAZARUS
WAS DEAD.
FOUR DAYS IN
THE TOMB.

MASTER, IF YOU
HAD BEEN HERE,
MY BROTHER WOULD
NOT BE DEAD.
MARTHA, LAZARUS
WILL RISE AGAIN.
OH, I KNOW HE WILL
RISE AGAIN ON THE
LAST DAY.
AT THE
RESURRECTION.

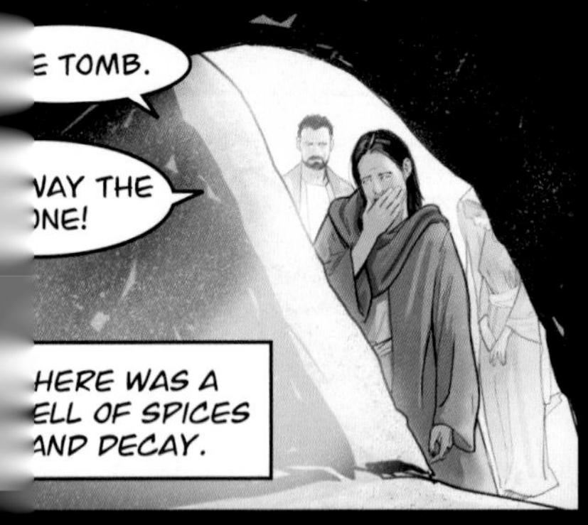

E TOMB.
VAY THE
ONE!
HERE WAS A
ELL OF SPICES
AND DECAY.

LAZARUS...
...COME OUT

LET HIM
GO FREE.

THE RETURN OF THE KING
JERUSALEM WAS IN SIGHT. IT WOULD SOON BE PASSOVER.
THE SON SENT TWO OF HIS DISCIPLES INTO THE VILLAGE AHEAD.
YOU'LL FIND A DONKEY TETHERED THERE. UNTIE IT AND BRING IT. SAY, "THE MASTER NEEDS IT".
WHAT ARE YOU DOING?
THE MASTER NEEDS IT.
IT WAS AS THE SON HAD SAID.
AND AS THE PROPHET ZECHARIAH HAD SAID CENTURIES BEFORE:
"LOOK!"
"YOUR KING COMES... RIDING ON A DONKEY."
"HE WILL TAKE AWAY WAR CHARIOTS AND HORSES. BOWS THAT WERE MADE FOR BATTLE WILL BE BROKEN..."
PEACE IN HEAVEN, GLORY TO GOD!
BLESSED IS HE WHO COMES AS KING IN GOD'S NAME!
"...HE WILL BRING PEACE TO NATIONS AND YOUR KING WILL RULE FROM SEA TO SEA..."
"...HIS KINGDOM WILL REACH ACROSS THE EARTH."
THE SON ENTERED JERUSALEM AND WENT TO THE TEMPLE.
NO ONE KNEW WHAT HE WOULD DO.

THE REBUILDER

TO BETRAY OR
TO LOVE?
JUDAS ISCARIOT, A DISCIPLE. A FRIEND OF THE SON. A LOVER OF HIS COUNTRY? A LOVER OF MONEY? WHATEVER THE REASON...
...JUDAS BECAME THE SON'S BETRAYER.
AS ARRANGED, THIRTY PIECES OF SILVER. YOU CAN HELP US FIND HIM?
I SAID SO.
GOOD...GOOD.
ALL WE HAVE TO DO...
...IS WAIT.
CAN WE TRUST HIM?
I THINK SO. FOR NOW, ANYWAY.
WHY IS HE SO DISILLUSIONED?
WHO KNOWS?
THE PASSOVER
THE SON AND HIS FRIENDS WERE AT SUPPER.
MY FRIENDS, I WILL ONLY BE WITH YOU FOR A LITTLE WHILE LONGER. AND THIS TIME, YOU CANNOT GO WHERE I AM GOING.
BUT I AM GIVING YOU A NEW COMMANDMENT: LOVE EACH OTHER AS I HAVE LOVED YOU. THEN EVERYONE WILL KNOW THAT YOU ARE MY DISCIPLES.
TAKE OFF YOUR SANDALS. I WILL WASH YOUR FEET.
THE SON TIED A TOWEL AROUND HIMSELF.
WHAT? NEVER!
LATER YOU WILL UNDERSTAND...AND IF I, YOUR MASTER, WASH YOUR FEET...
...YOU MUST WASH EACH OTHER'S.
SERVING AND LOVING ONE ANOTHER IS HOW PEOPLE WILL KNOW YOU ARE MY DISCIPLES.

THE BETRAYED
ONE OF YOU WILL BETRAY ME TONIGHT.
WHO WOULD DO THAT?
THE ONE I GIVE THIS PIECE OF BREAD TO.
I WILL NEVER BETRAY YOU, MASTER! NEVER! EVEN IF I HAVE TO DIE FOR YOU!
ROCK, THREE TIMES YOU WILL SAY THAT YOU DON'T EVEN KNOW ME. BEFORE THE ROOSTER CROWS AT DAWN.
JUDAS, TAKE THIS PIECE...
SO JUDAS, THE BETRAYER, SLIPPED OUT.
...BE QUICK ABOUT WHAT YOU ARE DOING.
DON'T BE WORRIED OR AFRAID. I GIVE YOU PEACE. PEACE THAT ONLY I CAN GIVE. IT ISN'T THE KIND OF PEACE THAT THE WORLD CAN GIVE. NOW...
...LET US GIVE THANKS. TAKE THIS BREAD AND EAT IT. THIS IS MY BODY, GIVEN FOR YOU.
TAKE THIS AND DRINK IT. THIS IS MY BLOOD, POURED OUT FOR YOU.
AND WITH IT, GOD MAKES A NEW COVENANT WITH YOU. SO THAT MANY PEOPLE WILL HAVE THEIR SINS FORGIVEN.
FROM NOW ON, I AM NOT GOING TO DRINK ANY WINE UNTIL I DRINK NEW WINE WITH YOU IN MY FATHER'S KINGDOM.

THE ABANDONED
THE SON WENT WITH HIS DISCIPLES TO A PLACE CALLED GETHSEMANE.
HE TOOK THE ROCK AND THE TWO BROTHERS, JAMES AND JOHN, TO PRAY.
I AM SO SAD THAT IT CRUSHES ME. I FEEL AS THOUGH I AM DYING.
STAY HERE WHILE I GO TO PRAY. AND KEEP AWAKE. KEEP WATCH FOR ME.
YES, MASTER.
WE WILL.
MY FATHER, IF IT IS POSSIBLE, DON'T MAKE ME SUFFER. PLEASE TAKE THIS CUP AWAY FROM ME.
BUT DO WHAT YOU WANT. NOT WHAT I WANT.
ASLEEP! COULDN'T YOU KEEP AWAKE AND WATCH FOR ONE HOUR?
OH, WE...ER...WE WERE JUST...
SORRY, MASTER, WE TRIED...
GET UP! THE TIME HAS COME.
THE SON OF MAN IS TO BE HANDED OVER TO SINFUL MEN. THE BETRAYER IS HERE.
MASTER!
MY FRIEND, WILL YOU BETRAY THE SON OF MAN WITH A KISS?

ALSE WITNESS
THE SON IS TAKEN TO THE HIGH PRIEST'S HOUSE.
MOVE... NOW!
COME ON...PEOPLE ARE WAITING!
HEY...
...WEREN'T YOU WITH THE SON FROM GALILEE?
WHAT? NO, I DON'T KNOW WHAT YOU'RE TALKING ABOUT!
LATER...
LOOK OVER THERE! YOU! WEREN'T YOU A FOLLOWER OF THE SON?
ME? NO, I DON'T KNOW ANYONE CALLED THE SON.
ARE YOU SURE? YOU LOOK LIKE ONE OF THEM.
AND YOUR ACCENT...YOU SOUND--
LOOK...
...HOW MANY TIMES DO I HAVE TO TELL YOU? I DON'T KNOW ANYONE CALLED THE SON!
"ROCK, THREE TIMES YOU WILL SAY THAT YOU DON'T EVEN KNOW ME..."
"...BEFORE THE ROOSTER CROWS AT DAWN."
MASTER!
MASTER, FORGIVE ME.

THE SON OF GOD?

JESUS, THE SON! WE HAVE HEARD SO MUCH ABOUT YOU.

IT APPEARS YOU CAN DESTROY THEN RAISE THE TEMPLE IN THREE DAYS. REMARKABLE... ASTOUNDING. HAVE YOU NO RESPONSE? MESSIAH?

BEFORE THE LIVING GOD, YOU MUST TELL THE TRUTH. ARE YOU THE MESSIAH? THE SON OF GOD? WELL, ARE YOU?

YOU SAY SO. BUT SOON YOU WILL SEE THE SON OF MAN SITTING AT THE RIGHT HAND OF GOD THE ALL-POWERFUL...

...AND COMING ON THE CLOUDS OF HEAVEN.

BLASPHEMY! THIS MAN CLAIMS TO BE GOD! HE ADMITS IT HIMSELF. HE IS GUILTY AND DESERVES TO DIE! TAKE HIM AWAY...

CONDEMNED

THE NEXT MORNING... BEFORE THE ROMAN GOVERNOR, PILATE

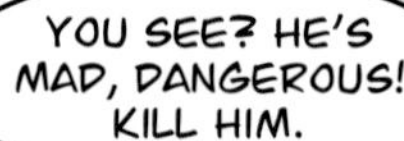

*DURING THE PASSOVER PILATE, **THE POLITICIAN**, ALWAYS FREED A PRISONER CHOSEN BY THE PEOPLE. AT THAT TIME A WELL-KNOWN REBEL NAMED BARABBAS WAS IN JAIL.*

THIS MAN, THE SON. I CANNOT FIND ANY REASON TO CONDEMN HIM. BUT, ACCORDING TO CUSTOM...

...ONE PRISONER CAN BE SET FREE. WHO SHALL IT BE?

THE SON, OR BARABBAS?

BARABBAS!

I HAVE DONE WRONG.
AH, BETRAYER...
WHAT IS THAT TO US? ENJOY YOUR MONEY. OR GIVE IT TO THE TEMPLE.
WHICH IS WHAT THE BETRAYER DID, THROWING IT AGAINST THE TEMPLE DOOR...
...BEFORE HANGING HIMSELF.
THE POLITICIAN HAD ORDERED THE SON TO BE FLOGGED.
REMEMBER HE'S THE KING! TRY NOT TO KILL HIM...
YET!
WHERE'S YOUR GOD NOW, YOUR HIGHNESS?
A CROWN.
FIT FOR A KING!
AND A ROBE OF PURPLE...A ROYAL ROBE FOR THE MESSIAH!
ALL HAIL THE KING!
THE KING!
THE SON, KING OF THE JEWS!

DEAD MAN WALKING
CRUCIFY HIM!
CRUCIFY HIM!
COME ON, "YOUR MAJESTY"!
GET UP!
SIMON, FROM CYRENE IN AFRICA, WASN'T LAUGHING OR JEERING.
HO! THE MESSIAH'S FINDING IT A BIT HARD.
CRUCIFY HIM!
TYPICAL ROYALTY...NO STAMINA!
WHAT ARE YOU WAITING FOR?
SEEING THIS, THE SOLDIERS FORCED HIM TO CARRY THE CROSS. WHICH HE DID, WILLINGLY.
WOMEN OF JERUSALEM, DON'T CRY FOR ME! CRY FOR YOURSELVES AND FOR YOUR CHILDREN.

KING OF THE JEWS

GOLGOTHA, WHICH MEANS "PLACE OF THE SKULL"

ALL RIGHT, KEEP STILL NOW. IT WILL BE WORSE IF WE HAVE TO DO IT TWICE.

TAKE A DEEP BREATH, YOUR HIGHNESS. THIS IS GOING TO...

THUD

AAARGHHH!

...HURT!

THEY CRUCIFIED HIM.
THIS IS JESUS, KING OF THE JEWS.
COME ON! YOU SAVED OTHERS. NOW SAVE YOURSELF.
IF YOU ARE THE SON OF GOD!

DARK NIGHT

IT WAS AFTERNOON...BUT DARKNESS FELL.

FATHER, FORGIVE THEM.

THEY DON'T KNOW WHAT THEY ARE DOING.

MY GOD, MY GOD! WHY HAVE YOU DESERTED ME?

FATHER, INTO YOUR HANDS I COMMEND MY SPIRIT.

IT IS FINISHED.

THE SON GAVE UP HIS SPIRIT AND DIED.

THE RESURRECTION AND THE LIFE

"MY LORD AND MY GOD!"
LATER...
THE UNFORGOTTEN ONE STOOD OUTSIDE THE TOMB WEEPING.
WOMAN! WHY DO YOU STAND AT THE TOMB WEEPING?
WHO ARE YOU LOOKING FOR?
THEY TOOK MY MASTER. AND I DON'T KNOW WHERE THEY PUT HIM.
IF YOU TOOK HIM, TELL ME WHERE YOU PUT HIM--
UNFORGOTTEN ONE!
MASTER!
DON'T HOLD ON TO ME! I HAVE NOT YET GONE TO THE FATHER. BUT GO TO MY DISCIPLES. SAY TO THEM...
...I AM RETURNING TO MY FATHER... YOUR FATHER.
TO MY GOD AND YOUR GOD.
THAT EVENING THE SON APPEARED TO HIS DISCIPLES.
PEACE BE WITH YOU!
THEY WERE OVERJOYED TO SEE THE SON WITH THEIR OWN EYES. ALL EXCEPT THOMAS, THE DOUBTER...
...WHO WASN'T THERE.
IMPOSSIBLE! UNTIL I SEE THE HOLES IN HIS HANDS, AND THE WOUND IN HIS SIDE, I WON'T BELIEVE IT.
DOUBTER! LOOK AT MY HANDS. TAKE YOUR HAND AND PUT IT IN MY SIDE. DON'T BE UNBELIEVING. BELIEVE!
MY LORD AND MY GOD!
SO YOU BELIEVE BECAUSE YOU'VE SEEN WITH YOUR OWN EYES.
EVEN BETTER BLESSINGS ARE IN STORE FOR THOSE WHO BELIEVE, WITHOUT SEEING.

ETERNAL KING
I HAVE BEEN GIVEN ALL AUTHORITY IN HEAVEN AND ON EARTH. GO AND SPREAD THE GOOD NEWS TO EVERYONE IN THE WORLD. MAKE DISCIPLES!
OVER FORTY DAYS THE SON APPEARED TO THE DISCIPLES.
BAPTIZE THEM IN THE NAME OF THE FATHER, THE SON, AND THE HOLY SPIRIT. TEACH THEM TO DO EVERYTHING I HAVE TOLD YOU.
YOU WILL RECEIVE POWER FROM THE HOLY SPIRIT AND YOU WILL BE MY WITNESSES THROUGHOUT THE EARTH.
I WILL BE WITH YOU ALWAYS.
EVEN UNTIL THE END OF THE WORLD.
AS THE DISCIPLES STOOD WATCHING, A VOICE CALLED TO THEM.
MEN FROM GALILEE, WHY ARE YOU HERE?
THE SON HAS BEEN TAKEN TO HEAVEN, BUT HE WILL RETURN IN THE SAME WAY YOU HAVE SEEN HIM GO.
SO THEY RETURNED TO JERUSALEM.

THE HOLY SPIRIT

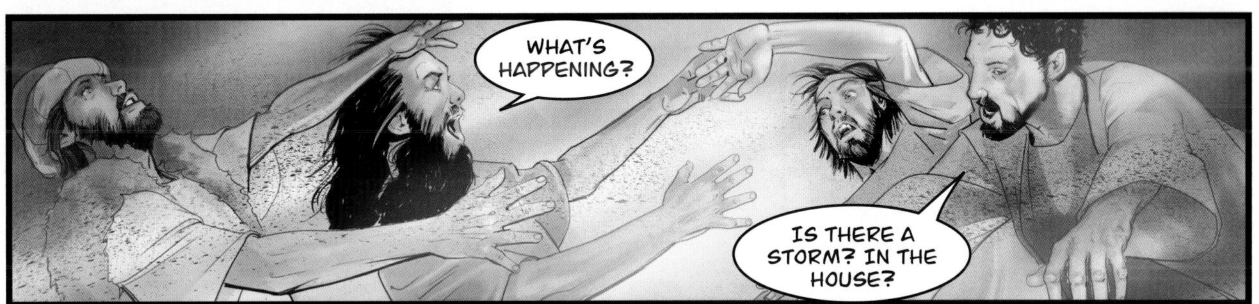

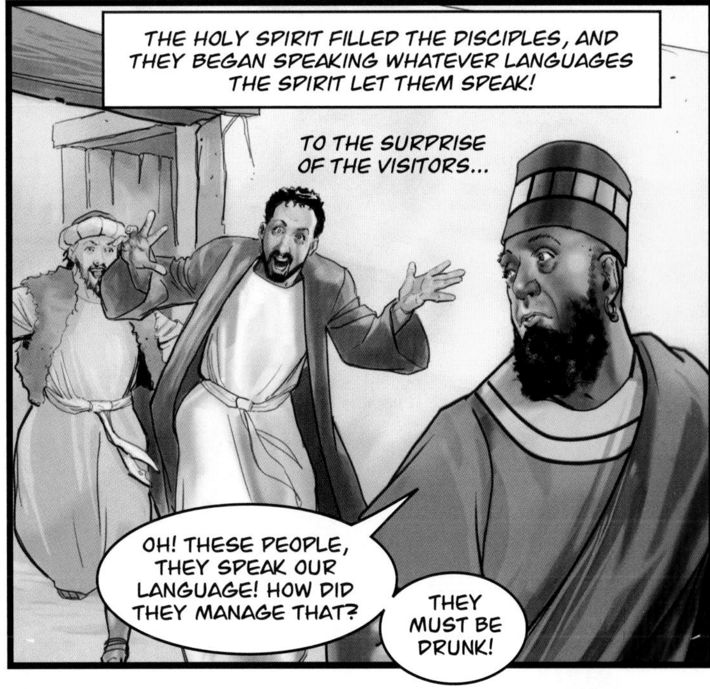

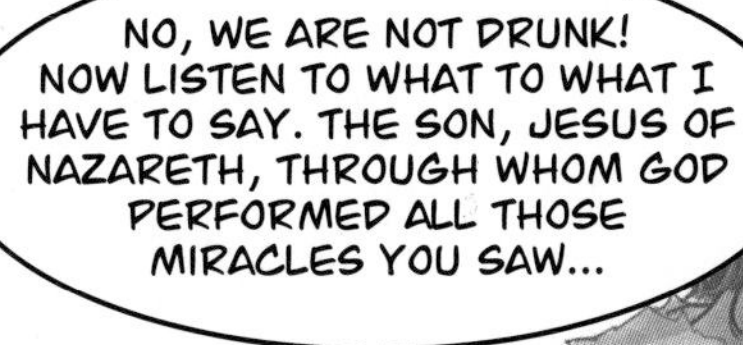

SOLID ROCK

MANY PEOPLE BEGAN TO BELIEVE IN THE SON AND WERE BAPTIZED. THEY JOINED THE DISCIPLES, SHARING THEIR BELONGINGS, AND OPENING THEIR HOMES TO PEOPLE IN NEED. EVERY DAY THEIR NUMBERS GREW.

ONE DAY, THE ROCK AND JOHN WENT TO THE TEMPLE. THEY CAME TO THE GATE KNOWN AS THE BEAUTIFUL GATE.

THE NEXT DAY...

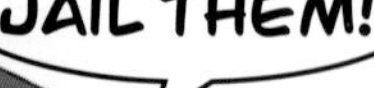

MAN OF FAITH

WAIT. NOT TOO HASTY! EVERYONE SAW WHAT HAPPENED. CAN WE DENY IT?
NO, I SUPPOSE NOT.
SO INSTEAD WE MUST STOP NEWS OF THIS "MIRACLE" SPREADING, YES?
YES, BUT HOW?
WE WARN THEM THEY MUST NOT DO ANYTHING IN THE NAME OF THIS MAN, JESUS, THE SON.
SO THE ROCK AND JOHN WERE RELEASED, TO THE CRIES OF PEOPLE PRAISING GOD.
THE COMMUNITY OF BELIEVERS GREW. SO GREAT WERE THEIR NUMBERS, NEW LEADERS WERE CHOSEN. ONE WAS A MAN NAMED STEPHEN, THE SERVER, WHO HELPED GIVE OUT FOOD TO THE POOR AND WIDOWS IN JERUSALEM.
A MAN OF FAITH AND WORKER OF MIRACLES, THE POWER OF THE SPIRIT SHONE POWERFULLY THROUGH HIM. BUT HIS ENEMIES INCREASED.
AH, SERVER, WELCOME. NOW, GIVING FOOD TO THE POOR IS...
...COMMENDABLE, ADMIRABLE! BUT IS IT TRUE WHAT WE HEAR? YOU HATE LAW MAN? HATE THE LAWS OF OUR PEOPLE? HATE GOD?
MY BROTHERS. MY FATHERS. ALL THROUGH OUR HISTORY OUR GREAT LEADERS HAVE TRIED TO POINT OUR PEOPLE TO GOD. TIME AND TIME AGAIN WE DIDN'T LISTEN. WE TURNED FROM GOD. BOWED DOWN TO IDOLS...
...EVEN KILLED PROPHETS. BUT YOU ARE WORSE. YOU REFUSED TO LISTEN TO GOD'S MESSIAH!
YOU SEIZED THE SON AND MURDERED HIM!
NOW I SEE HIM, STANDING AT GOD'S RIGHT HAND.
ENOUGH!
YOUR BLASPHEMY CONDEMNS YOU!
STONE HIM!

PERSECUTOR

SAUL, **THE PERSECUTOR**, WAS A MAN OF GREAT LEARNING. A MAN WHO HATED THE FOLLOWERS OF THE SON.

WHO IMPRISONED AND MURDERED THEM. AND WAS FEARED BY ALL.

NOW, UNDER THE HIGH PRIEST'S AUTHORITY, THE PERSECUTOR WAS TRAVELING TO DAMASCUS TO ARREST ANY FOLLOWERS HE COULD FIND THERE.

PERSECUTOR!

WHO ARE YOU, LORD?

I AM THE SON. THE ONE YOU ARE PERSECUTING. GET UP NOW AND GO INTO THE CITY. SOMEONE WILL TELL YOU WHAT YOU MUST DO.

I CAN'T SEE...

MASTER, ARE YOU ALL RIGHT? THAT VOICE, THE LIGHT...

DAMASCUS, JUST GET ME TO DAMASCUS.

FREED!

THE BIG GATE OPENED OF ITS OWN ACCORD.

AND SUDDENLY THE ROCK FOUND HIMSELF ALONE.

AND ALTHOUGH PERSECUTION OF THE CHURCH IN JERUSALEM INCREASED, THE GOSPEL SPREAD FURTHER AND FURTHER.

GRACE MAN

IN DAMASCUS, THE PERSECUTOR SAT BLIND FOR THREE DAYS.
ANANIAS CAME TO HIM.
THE SON SENT ME SO THAT YOU MAY SEE AGAIN...
...AND BE FILLED WITH THE HOLY SPIRIT.
IMMEDIATELY THE PERSECUTOR WAS HEALED...
JESUS IS THE SON OF GOD! HE IS RISEN FROM THE DEAD!
...AND WAS RENAMED PAUL, GRACE MAN. HE TRAVELED FAR AND WIDE. EVERYWHERE HE WENT PEOPLE BEGAN TO FOLLOW THE SON.
IN PHILIPPI, AT THE HOME OF LYDIA, THE HOUSEHOLD WAS BAPTIZED. BUT GRACE MAN WAS BEING WATCHED...
SERVANTS OF THE MOST HIGH GOD!
...BY A SLAVE-GIRL, TROUBLED BY A SPIRIT WHICH ENABLED HER TO PREDICT THE FUTURE.
IN THE NAME OF THE SON, LEAVE THIS WOMAN!
SHE'S FREE. THE SPIRIT HAS GONE.
YES. BUT SHE'S STILL A SLAVE. SHE MADE HER OWNER A LOT OF MONEY. HE MIGHT NOT BE HAPPY...
...HE WASN'T.
THESE JEWS ARE TEACHING CUSTOMS AGAINST OUR LAWS. THROW THEM IN JAIL!
GRACE MAN WAS PUT IN PRISON...
...WITH HIS FRIEND SILAS. THEY SANG AND PRAYED TO GOD.
LATER THAT NIGHT...
EARTHQUAKE! WHERE ARE THE PRISONERS?
DON'T WORRY, NO ONE HAS ESCAPED.
DID YOUR GOD DO THIS? WHAT MUST I DO TO BE SAVED?
YES. BELIEVE IN THE SON.
THE JAILER WAS BAPTIZED. AND GRACE MAN AND SILAS WERE FREED.

CITIZEN
DURING HIS TRAVELS, GRACE MAN FACED MUCH OPPOSITION FROM THE JEWISH LEADERS. THEY ATTEMPTED TO PUT HIM ON TRIAL.
AS A ROMAN CITIZEN, GRACE MAN INSISTED ON HIS RIGHT TO DEFEND HIMSELF IN ROME. AND SO HE SET SAIL. DAY AFTER DAY HIS SHIP BATTLED AGAINST HEAVY STORMS.
WHICH FINALLY BROKE IT APART.
DON'T GIVE UP HOPE. GOD PROMISED I WOULD STAND BEFORE THE EMPEROR IN ROME.
CLINGING TO THE WRECKAGE THEY WERE WASHED UP ON THE SHORE.
WE DID IT! JUST AS YOU SAID.
I TOLD YOU, GOD PROMISED. HE HAS PLANS FOR US.
THEY HAD LANDED ON MALTA. AS THEY GATHERED FOR WARMTH, ISLANDERS CAME TO HELP. BRINGING DRY CLOTHES AND FOOD.
AFTER THREE MONTHS, GRACE MAN SET SAIL FOR ROME.
WHEN HE ARRIVED, HE WAS ALLOWED TO LIVE IN A RENTED HOUSE WITH A GUARD FOR TWO YEARS. HE KNEW HE WAS GOING TO DIE, AND WROTE:
"THE TIME HAS COME FOR ME TO LEAVE THIS WORLD. I HAVE FOUGHT THE GOOD FIGHT. I HAVE FINISHED THE RACE. I HAVE KEPT THE FAITH. NOW A PRIZE IS WAITING FOR ME: THE CROWN OF RIGHTEOUSNESS. THE LORD WHO JUDGES RIGHTLY WILL GIVE IT TO ME ON THAT DAY. AND TO EVERYONE ELSE WHO ALSO LONGS FOR HIS COMING."

REVELATION MAN

PATMOS

JOHN'S HOME AND PRISON

WHY AM I HERE? FOR WHAT CRIME?

FOR SPEAKING OF THE SON, THE RULER OF THE KINGS OF THE EARTH.

THEY THINK I AM ALONE. BUT THE HOLY SPIRIT IS MY COMPANION, MY HELP AND GUIDE.

JOHN, **THE REVEALER**, SAT WAITING FOR THE SON TO RETURN. TO END SUFFERING. END TEARS. THEN HE HEARD A VOICE.

REVEALER!

WRITE IN A BOOK WHAT YOU SEE. THEN SEND IT TO THE SEVEN CHURCHES. DO NOT BE AFRAID!

I SAW A SCROLL CLOSED WITH **SEVEN** SEALS.

WHO IS WORTHY TO BREAK THE SEALS AND OPEN THE SCROLL?

LOOK! THE LION OF THE TRIBE OF JUDAH! HE CAN OPEN THE SEALS.

THEN I SAW THAT THE LION HAD CHANGED. I SAW IN ITS PLACE A LAMB, WEAK AND HELPLESS, WHO OPENED THE SEALS.

AT THE OPENING OF THE FIFTH SEAL THE MARTYRS CRIED, "HOW LONG BEFORE YOU JUDGE AND AVENGE OUR BLOOD?"
WHEN THE SIXTH SEAL WAS OPENED, THERE WAS A GREAT EARTHQUAKE. THE SUN TURNED BLACK, THE MOON TURNED RED, AND STARS FELL FROM THE SKY...
...AND KINGS, THE RICH AND POWERFUL, AND EVERYONE, SLAVE OR FREE, TOOK REFUGE IN CAVES.
HIDE US FROM THE ONE SEATED ON THE THRONE.
FOUR ANGELS STOOD AT THE FOUR CORNERS OF THE WORLD HOLDING BACK THE FOUR WINDS.
AND THEN...I HEARD A SONG AS IF FROM A VAST CROWD OF PEOPLE SINGING, "SALVATION BELONGS TO OUR GOD! AND IT COMES FROM THE LAMB OF GOD!"

WHEN THE LAMB OPENED THE SEVENTH SEAL, THERE WAS SILENCE IN HEAVEN...
...AND A SIGN APPEARED IN THE HEAVENS: A WOMAN IN LABOR.
SHE CRIED OUT AS SHE WAS SOON TO GIVE BIRTH.
THEN I SAW ANOTH A HUGE DRAGON SEVEN HEADS AP IN THE HEAVE
IT STOOD IN FRONT WOMAN, READY TO THE CHILD AS SOO WAS BORN.
BUT THE CHILD RESCUED, AND THE FLED INTO THE DE
AND THERE WAS WAR IN HEAVEN.
MICHAEL AND HIS ANGE FOUGHT AGAINST THE DRAGON AND HIS ANGEL
AND THE GREAT DRAGON, THE ACCUSER, AND HIS ANGELS WERE HURLED TO THE EARTH.
IN ANGER, THE DRAGON PURSUED THE WOMAN AN HER CHILDREN, THOSE WHO OBEYED GOD'S COMMAN AND HELD TO THE TESTIMONY OF THE SON.

BABYLON BURNED.
I SAW IT! AND WATCHING
IT, UNDERSTOOD.
THIS CITY WAS THE HEART
OF THE EVIL EMPIRE. AND
STOOD ON **SEVEN** HILLS.

LOOKING THROUGH THE SMOKE,
I SAW THE HEAVENS OPEN.

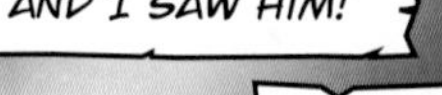
AND I SAW HIM!
THE LORD! THE
FAITHFUL AND
TRUE ONE.
KING OF KINGS AND
LORD OF LORDS.
RIDING A WHITE HORSE, THE
ARMIES OF HEAVEN BEHIND HIM.
BRINGING JUSTICE
FOR EVERYONE.

THEN, COMING DOWN
FROM HEAVEN...
...MICHAEL THE ARCHANGEL WITH THE KEY
TO HELL AND HOLDING A GREAT CHAIN.
THE ACCUSER WAS BOUND AND
THROWN INTO THE BOTTOMLESS PIT.
IT WAS SEALED, SO HE
COULD DECEIVE THE
NATIONS NO MORE.

KINGDOM COME!

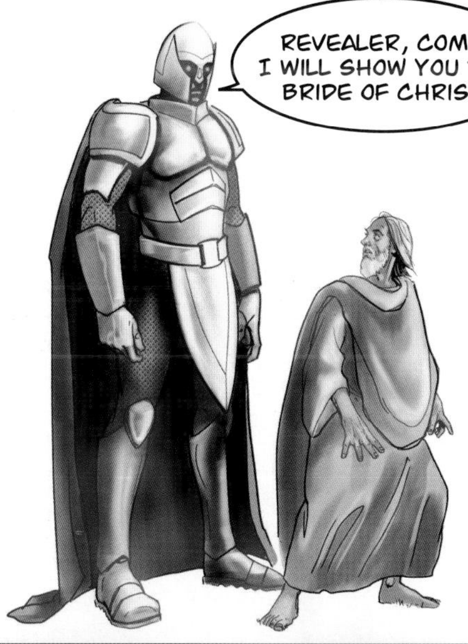

REVEALER, I AM MAKING ALL THINGS NEW...HEALING ALL THE NATIONS.

IT IS DONE! I AM THE BEGINNING AND THE END.

COME! EVERYONE WHO IS THIRSTY. COME AND DRINK THE FREE GIFT OF THE WATER OF LIFE.

I AM COMING AGAIN SOON!

AMEN! COME, SON OF GOD!

BIBLE REFERENCES

OLD TESTAMENT

NEW TESTAMENT

PUBLISHED BY LION BOOKS
AN IMPRINT OF
LION HUDSON PLC
WILKINSON HOUSE, JORDAN HILL ROAD,
OXFORD OX2 8DR, ENGLAND
WWW.LIONHUDSON.COM/HEROBIBLE
ISBN 978 0 7459 5617 6
FIRST EDITION 2015

TO NATHAN – A FUTURE HERO – FROM THE TEAM!

ACKNOWLEDGMENTS
CREATIVE CONCEPT: ED CHATELIER, THE EDGE GROUP
ILLUSTRATORS: SIKU (OT), JEFF ANDERSON (NT)
TEXT: RICHARD THOMAS, JEFF ANDERSON, ED CHATELIER
LETTERING: RICHARD THOMAS
COMMISSIONING EDITORS: BECKI BRADSHAW AND ANDREW HODDER-WILLIAMS
EDITORS: JESS TINKER AND VIC TEBBS
DESIGNERS: JUDE MAY AND JONATHAN ROBERTS
PRODUCTION: KYLIE ORD

A CATALOGUE RECORD FOR THIS BOOK IS AVAILABLE FROM THE BRITISH LIBRARY
PRINTED AND BOUND IN POLAND, AUGUST 2015, LH44